Media and the moving image

John Mannion

Published by Letts Educational
The Chiswick Centre
414 Chiswick High Road
London W4 5TF

📞 020 89963333
📠 020 87428390
✉ mail@lettsed.co.uk
🌐 www.letts-education.com

Letts Educational Limited is a division of Granada
Learning Limited, part of Granada plc.

ISBN 1 84085 880X

British Library Cataloguing in Publication Data
A catalogue record for this book is available from the
British Library.

Developed and packaged by McLean Press Ltd

Commissioned by Helen Clark

Project management by Vicky Butt and Julia Swales

Edited by Rachel Harrison

Cover design by bigtop, Bicester, UK

Internal design by bigtop, Bicester, UK

Illustrations by Linda Combi, Paul McCaffrey and
Darren Lingard

Production by PDQ

Printed and bound by Canale, Italy

Acknowledgements

The authors and publishers wish to thank the following for permission
to use copyright material:

1066 and all that cover on page 11 courtesy of Methuen; 2nd mice
news item on pages 69–70 courtesy of spaced.co.uk/Merchant Internet;
3rd mice news item on page 70 © NME/IPC Magazines; Academic
gaming web article on page 78 courtesy of Jorgen Kirksaether; ASH logo
on page 89 courtesy of ASH; bbc billboard on page 91 courtesy BBC;
bbci review on page 79 courtesy bbc.co.uk; Benetton '3 Hearts'
advertisement on page 107 © Corbis; *Bliss* magazine cover and photo
shoot on pages 29–30 © Bliss/EMAP; *Blush!* magazine cover and photo
shoot on pages 29–30 © H Bauer Publishing 2002 and reproduced with
permission. (*Blush!* is published fortnightly in the UK. Blush! now cost
£1.60. Contact: blush.mag@bauer.co.uk); Car advertisement on page
106 courtesy of Mazda UK; Characters from *Diablo II* on page 77
courtesy of planetdiablo.com; *Charles Dickens: A Beginner's Guide* cover
on page 50 courtesy of Headway; Cinderella image 1 on page 5 ©
Topham; Cinderella image 2 on page 5 © Mary Evans Picture Library;
Computer game *Myst* image on page 71 © Cyan Worlds, Inc. All rights
reserved No part may be copied or reproduced without express, written
permission of Cyan Worlds, Inc.; Dambusters article on pages 110–111
Crown copyright/Deltaweb International; *Dickens* cover on page 50
courtesy of Mandarin; Dickens dictionary entry on page 49 courtesy of
Collins Education; Dickens encyclopedia entry on page 49 courtesy of
Microsoft Corporation; Dickens website page on page 49 courtesy of
Mitsuharu Matsuoka, University of Nagoya, Japan; *Empire* magazine
cover on page 81 © Empire/EMAP; Fog index web item on pages 57–58
courtesy of McLellan Wyatt Digital; Fog news item on page 57 courtesy
of *The Daily Telegraph*; FOREST logo on page 89 courtesy of FOREST;
images from the film *Frankenstein* (1957) featuring Peter Cushing and
Christopher Lee on page 97 courtesy of BFI Stills Archive; Greenpeace
article and photograph on pages 85–86 © Greenpeace; Guardian
computer games article on page 77 courtesy of Guardian Media Group;
Guardian Unlimited web search on page 26 courtesy of Guardian Media
Group; Hamfind web search page on page 26 courtesy of Hamfind;
Health Matters article on pages 91–92 courtesy of Health Matters; 'I
Join the Regiment' from *Adolf Hitler, My Part in his Downfall* by Spike
Milligan on pages 109–110 courtesy of Spike Milligan Productions; Kids
show transcript on page 21 courtesy of forkidssakeradio.com; Mice news
item on pages 66–67 courtesy of bbc.co.uk; extract from *Mort* by Terry
Pratchett on page 62 © Terry Pratchett/Gollancz Orion; National Anti-
Vivisection Society leaflet on pages 37–39 courtesy of NAVS; O^2
advertisement on page 107 courtesy of O^2; Observer article on pages
102–103 courtesy of Guardian Media Group; Photograph of girl on tank
on page 32 © David Turnley/Corbis; *Presenting the Past* contents page
and extract on pages 12–13 courtesy of Collins Education; *Real* contents
pages on page 82 © Real/H Bauer Publishing Ltd; SAD website article
on page 45 courtesy of outsidein.co.uk; Scriptwriting extracts on pages
53–54 courtesy of Andrew Medurst, University of Sussex; *Shrek* image
on page 42 © Topham; *Shrek* review from bfi.co.uk on page 41 courtesy
of British Film Institute; *Shrek* review from the Observer on page 42
courtesy of Guardian Media Group; Smoke Free Movies advertisement on
page 90 courtesy of Professor Stanton Glantz, University of California;
Sony VAIO advertisment on page 106 courtesy of Sony UK/Sony Vaio
UK; *Stormin' Normans* cover, contents page and extract on pages 11–13
courtesy of Scholastic/Terry Deary; *The Oxford Reader's Companion to
Dickens* cover on page 50 courtesy of Oxford University Press; *The Thief
of Always* extract by Clive Barker on page 44 courtesy of Collins
Education; *Total DVD* magazine contents pages on 82 courtesy of Total
DVD magazine/Highbury House Communications plc; Walkers Lites
advertisement on page 108 courtesy of Walkers; Washington 1968
image on pages 33–34 © Marc Riboud/Magnum.

Contents

What is the media?

Aims

- To revise your knowledge of the media.
- To expand your understanding of what **media texts** involve.

Starter session

Like all words, 'media' has a range of meanings. With a partner, decide on an order of importance for the following meanings in the context of your English lessons:

- place where ancient Medes lived
- what something is made from, as in a 'mixed-media' artwork
- the press and television
- something that contains or holds something else.

Introduction

In studying the media we are less concerned with the story or other information than we are with the way it is conveyed.

1 If you think of the story 'Cinderella', do you think of:
- the words on the page?
- the events in the story?
- the shots in the cartoon?
- the sounds of the reader on the tape?
- the pictures in the book?

2 Only one of the above responses is not concerned with the **medium** in which the story exists. Discuss which one it is with a partner.

3 Also with your partner, discuss whether it is possible to think of 'just' a story, or whether we always think of stories as they happen in films or books.

4 Write a brief account of how you first encountered the story of either 'Cinderella' or any other well-known fairy tale.

Development

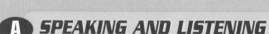

A **SPEAKING AND LISTENING** READING **WRITING**

Who produced this text and why?

1 Who might produce the following texts:
- a programme for a local radio station?
- a pop song?
- a full-page advertisement in a national newspaper?
- a shopping list?
- a Hollywood film?
- a personal weblog?

2 Why might each of these texts have been produced?

3 In 2001, the first novel to be sponsored by a firm of jewellers was published. Discuss with your partner whether you would respond differently to a novel if you knew that it had been sponsored. Would it make any difference who the sponsors were (e.g. Cadbury's chocolate or the World Health Organisation)?

B *SPEAKING AND LISTENING* READING *WRITING*

What type of text is it?

1 With a partner, discuss in what type of media text you might find the following features:

- headlines
- sound effects
- words arranged in alphabetical order
- pen and ink drawings used to tell a story
- pictures and writing giving information
- a story in writing only.

2 Different media texts have different conventions or rules. Match the following rules or conventions with the correct type of writing.

Should have a beginning, middle and end.

Can use bullet points for emphasis.

Can use rhyme.

Places the most important information first.

Always starts with an address.

newspaper article

poem   letter

information text

short story

C *SPEAKING AND LISTENING* READING *WRITING*

How is it produced?

1 Write a list of the following texts in order, from the least expensive to produce to the most expensive:

- a personal home page on the Internet
- a blockbuster movie
- a novel
- a fanzine
- a television advertisement.

2 Which of the following methods of advertising is most likely to convince you that you are buying a high-quality product? Why? Write a brief passage explaining your answer.

- A national television advertising campaign.
- A hand-written advertisement in a shop window.
- An advertisement in a local newspaper.

3 Discuss with a partner whether texts produced by large numbers of people are more or less likely to be trustworthy. For instance, are you more or less likely to trust an information text produced by a major publisher than something published by one individual on the Internet? Share your views with the class.

D   **READING**   **WRITING**

How does it create meaning?

Different media create meanings in different ways. Some use words on a printed page, others use sounds, and others use pictures or a combination of words, sounds and pictures.

THE WAR OF THE WORLDS RADIO BROADCAST

On Hallowe'en, October 31, 1938, Orson Welles' Mercury Theater broadcast a radio version of H.G. Wells' story of an attack from Mars, called *The War of the Worlds*. The broadcast began as a programme of dance music, but this was soon interrupted by an apparently live broadcast from Grovers Mill, New Jersey, describing the arrival of the Martians and their horrific behaviour. The reporter on the scene seemed to be in great fear as he moved around the area giving graphic descriptions of terrible events. The result was panic on the east coast of America, with people fleeing their homes, going into hiding or arming themselves with whatever weapons came to hand.

1 What features of the broadcast caused people to respond in panic?

2 Assuming that Orson Welles did not want to cause an invasion scare, why do think he presented the story as he did?

3 Do you think people would react in the same way today if a television company transmitted an extremely realistic version of an invasion? If not, why not?

4 How did the producers exploit the main features of the medium of radio to create the desired effect on the audience?

Who is the audience for the text?

As the story about The *War of the Worlds* shows, some media texts can have a very powerful effect on an audience. Audiences can also have a very powerful effect on the media.

1 How might the need to obtain a PG certificate affect the decisions made by a film maker?

2 Most chart singles are bought by 9- to 14-year-olds. How does this affect the kind of music that is released by record companies?

3 What is the 'nine o'clock watershed' on television? How does it affect TV schedules?

4 Explain why a company such as Nike might or might not choose each of the following places as an advertising site:

- Classic FM
- in the commercial break during a football match on ITV
- *Good Housekeeping* magazine
- *The Daily Telegraph*
- on a billboard in Oxford Street, London.

In any piece of writing, the style will be affected by the intended audience.

5 Which audiences do you think the following pieces of writing are intended for?

6 What features of the writing gave you clues about the intended audience?

Learning how to browse the Web faster and more easily

If you learn just a few basic things about browsing the Web, such as how to use the buttons on the Internet Explorer toolbar, you'll find that browsing the Web is easier and faster. To start browsing the Web, click any link on your home page, which is the page that appears when you start Internet Explorer. You can see whether an item on a page is a link by moving the mouse pointer over the item. If the pointer changes to a hand, the item is a link. A link can be a picture, a 3-D image, or colored text (usually underlined). Now you're ready to find a website on your own.

http//www.herdofnerds.info is a really simple example of a web address. The 'http' bit tells you that the address is for a web page. The 'www' stands for World Wide Web (as if you didn't know!), the 'herdofnerds' bit tells you the name of the 'host' organisation supplying the web pages, while '.info' indicates that it is a document or bunch of documents published by an information organisation.

How does the text present its subject?

This area of the media is often quite controversial. Any given text will have a 'story', but along with this there will be underlying attitudes and ideas that the producers of the text might not have thought about.

With a partner, discuss the underlying messages that could be read into the following texts:

- a film in which a male hero rescues a woman in distress
- a business magazine in which women are referred to only in their roles as secretaries or personal assistants
- a television programme set in London with a large cast which does not feature a single black actor
- films that only feature black people as criminals or in minor roles
- a book in which all the working-class characters seem to be lazy or irresponsible
- news items that only ever mention the third world when there is a natural disaster or a famine.

Review

As a class, discuss why the media is so important in our lives today. Think about the different types of media we are exposed to and the ways that we can respond to them.

Homework

Write two paragraphs explaining which of the media you think is the most important today and why you think this is.

Choosing information texts

Aims

- To find the information you need for a given task.
- To find relevant information in the resources you choose, using skim reading, indexes, **glossaries** and **key words**.

Starter session

As your teacher reads out the following questions, write down your responses.

Where would you:

- look up the meaning of a word?
- find information about your favourite pop star?
- find out extra information for a geography project?
- read about recent events?
- work out your route for a walk in the country?
- find a list of words that have similar meanings to one you have in mind?
- find out about events that occurred in the year of your birth?

KEY WORDS

A **glossary** is an alphabetical list of words, together with their meanings. You often find glossaries in information books, which use lots of technical words which might be unfamiliar to the reader.

Key words are words it is important to know the meaning of. They are often highlighted within a text.

Introduction

It has often been said that we live in an information age. It is certainly true that the number of ways of accessing information has increased dramatically in the last century and a half. We can see this if we think back to 1851, the year of the Great Exhibition of Victorian science and technology.

With a partner, discuss which of the following media you think were available in that year*:

- CD-Roms ● film ● Internet ● photographs ● radio
- sound recordings ● telephones ● video.

The problem today is not so much where to find information, but which source of information best suits our needs. This will depend on circumstances. In the rest of this unit we will look at how to choose the right information text and how to find the information you need in it.

Development

A *SPEAKING AND LISTENING* ~~READING~~ ~~WRITING~~

With a partner, discuss the following questions.

1 When is a book better than the Internet?
2 When is a dictionary better than an encyclopaedia?
3 When is the Internet better than a newspaper?

B *SPEAKING AND LISTENING* *READING* ~~WRITING~~

Choosing books starts when we look at their covers. Imagine you are going to do some research for a project on the Norman invasion of England in 1066. With a partner, discuss the following questions.

1 Which of these books do you think will provide the most information?
2 What features of the cover help you to choose a book that will be most useful to you?
3 Which book are you most likely to get in a school classroom?

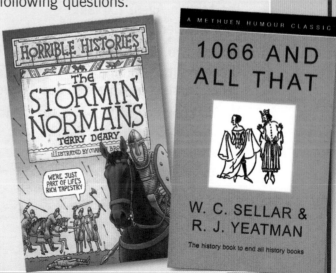

* Only photographs – first accounts of photography were made public in 1839.

One good way of deciding whether a book is useful is to look at the contents page. Here are the contents pages of two books on this period: *The Stormin' Normans* and *Presenting the Past*.

CONTENTS

Contents

1 Which of the two texts do you think will give the clearest picture of life in the Middle Ages? Explain your answer.

2 Do the two books cover broadly similar areas?
What connections can you see between the two?

3 Which book do you think will be the most entertaining? Explain your answer.

Here are two extracts from these books. With a partner, compare the two extracts.

SOURCE 5 Written about 60 years after the events described, by a monk trained in Normandy

66 *The royal forces approached York, only to learn that the Danes had fled. The King ordered his men to repair the castles in the city. He himself continued to comb forests and remote mountainous places, stopping at nothing to hunt out the enemy hidden there. He cut down many in his vengeance; destroyed the lairs of others; harried the land, and burned homes to ashes. Nowhere else had William shown such cruelty. He made no effort to control his fury and punished the innocent with the guilty. In his anger he ordered that all crops, herds and food of every kind should be brought together and burned to ashes, so that the whole region north of the Humber might be stripped of all means of sustenance. As a result of this such a terrible famine fell upon the humble and defenceless people that more than 100,000 Christian folk of both sexes, young and old alike, perished of hunger.* 99

1 Which gives the most information?

2 Which is the most entertaining?

3 Do you think it is appropriate to make jokes about a form of genocide (the mass killing of a whole group of people)?

4 Neither text uses the words of somebody who was present at the event. Which account do you think is most likely to be historically accurate? Share your ideas with the rest of the class.

5 Which of these two texts would you use if you were doing a History project? Write a brief explanation of your reasons.

William set off to sort out the nuisance in the north. He didn't just want to win. He wanted to destroy them so completely they would never rebel again. What he did became known as 'The Harrying of the North'.

The Vikings left York before William could catch them…

William set about destroying the northern region as he marched through it. Every English male was murdered.

The houses and the barns were burned. The farm animals were killed so there was nothing left for the people to eat.

Corpses were left to rot by the side of the roads and the desperate English survivors ate them to stay alive…

Horrible Histories Health Warning: Eating dead bodies you find in a ditch can damage your health. So don't do it.

Disease came along to add to the misery of the survivors. The northern towns and villages were still struggling to recover years later.

The North certainly didn't revolt again. The Conqueror's cruelty worked.

Twenty years after 'The Harrying of the North' William the Conqueror started to feel bad about his cruelty. It's said he was dead sorry … unlike the English who were simply dead dead.

The stuffed saint
When the Norman kingdom had settled, over 30 years later, they brought Cuthbert back to Durham to put him in the new cathedral the Normans were building there.

How we access texts is very important. *The Stormin' Normans* has a contents page but it doesn't have an index. *Presenting the Past* has both an index and a contents page.

1 What is the advantage of being able to use an index in an information text?

2 What does the presence or absence of an index tell us about how the authors thought their books would be used?

If you are looking for an exact piece of information in a book, there are several possible ways of finding it. The diagram below shows a possible strategy.

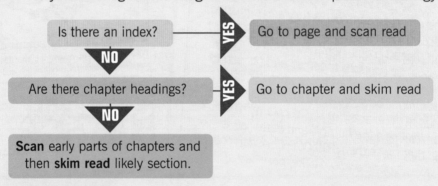

Is there an index? — **YES** → Go to page and scan read

NO ↓

Are there chapter headings? — **YES** → Go to chapter and skim read

NO ↓

Scan early parts of chapters and then **skim read** likely section.

KEY TERMS

Scanning a text is when you quickly move your eyes over it, looking for the information you want.

Skim reading is when you read the important bits of a text, usually the first sentence of a paragraph, until you find a relevant section.

Which strategy would you use to find out about, say, the death of William II in *The Stormin' Normans*?

Review

As a class, discuss what advice you would give to the publishers of texts such as *The Stormin' Normans* to make their books more useful for research.

Homework

Write a brief account of an information text you have used recently and discuss how well it worked as a research tool.

Words and pictures

Aims

- To compare and contrast the ways information is presented.

Starter session

Discuss with your class which of the following strategies you prefer to use if you need to go somewhere new. Notice that they are all different strategies to achieve the same task.

- I like to have a map marked with the best route.
- I like to have written directions which point out landmarks and buildings.
- I can usually remember directions once I have heard them.
- I like to get near to where I am supposed to be going and then ask.
- I prefer a map and written directions.
- I prefer to take a taxi or get someone to give me lift.

Introduction

When we talk about the media we are interested in the way information is presented rather than in the information itself. It is possible to present the same piece of information in different media, and also to use different forms of presentation within any one medium. The way in which the information is presented can affect how well the audience receives it.

Development

A **SPEAKING AND LISTENING**   **READING**   *WRITING*

Read this account of the water cycle.

The Hydrological Cycle

Water exists in three states: liquid, gaseous (water vapour or steam) and solid (snow and ice). It can also pass from one state to another by freezing, melting, condensing and evaporating. New water is not created on the Earth's surface or in its atmosphere; nor is 'old' water lost. Rather, there is a finite amount, and this circulates in what is known as *the hydrological cycle*. Water moves around the cycle both by physically moving and by changing its states as the diagram shows.

Today, 97% of the water in the hydrological cycle is contained in the world's seas, oceans and saline lakes. The remaining 3% is fresh water. About 75% of all fresh water is contained in glaciers and ice sheets, and just over 24% is groundwater (i.e. underground). The rivers, lakes, soil and atmosphere therefore contain a very small amount (less than 0.5%) of the world's fresh water at any one time

During glacial periods of the Earth's history the amount of water contained in ice sheets and glaciers has been greater, and the amount in oceans smaller.

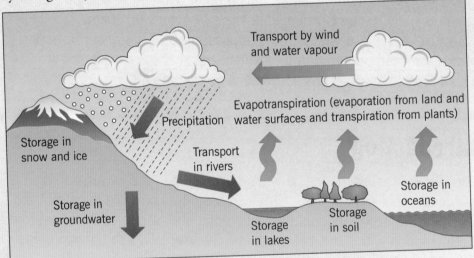

Transport by wind and water vapour

Precipitation

Storage in snow and ice

Evapotranspiration (evaporation from land and water surfaces and transpiration from plants)

Transport in rivers

Storage in groundwater

Storage in lakes

Storage in soil

Storage in oceans

With a partner, discuss the following questions.

1 Which part of the above account did you find the most useful – the text or the diagram?

2 Do you think you would have understood the text without the diagram?

3 Could you have understood the diagram without the text?

4 Was everything in the diagram contained in the text?

5 Was everything in the text contained in the diagram?

The text also describes the proportions of fresh water distribution in the different parts of the water cycle. Here are two different ways of representing this information.

Table

Fresh water	Percentage
Glaciers and ice sheets	75
Groundwater	24
Rivers, lakes, soil and atmosphere	0.5

Graph

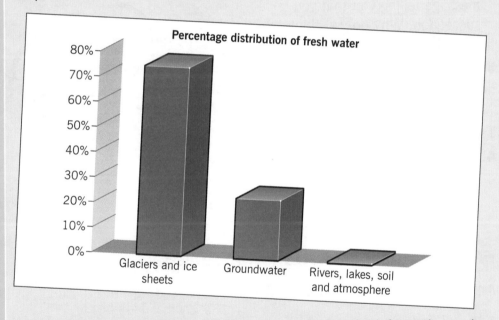

1 Write about which of these two ways of presenting the information makes it clearer. Which allows you to access the information the most quickly?

2 Present the information about the relative proportions of fresh and salt water in the hydrological cycle as both a table and a diagram.

3 Write down two suggestions for how you might present information about the water cycle using a computer or on television. Discuss your suggestions with the rest of the class.

One of the advantages computers have over the printed page is that they allow us to move things around. Here is a web page that turns the water cycle into a sort of jigsaw puzzle.

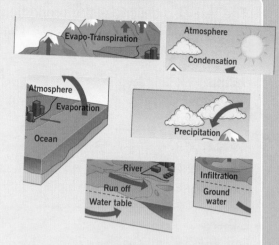

1 Look carefully at the pieces of the puzzle and see if you could solve it.

2 When doing the puzzle online, every time you place a piece of the puzzle correctly you get a message telling you that you have succeeded. Why do you think the page designers have done this?

3 Write a sentence or two about whether or not you prefer your learning to be interactive.

The completed puzzle looks like this.

4 How does this diagram compare with the one on page 16?

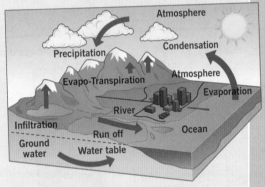

A third diagram looks like this.

1 Which style do you prefer? Discuss with a partner.

2 Which diagram seems to be the clearest and most accurate? Compare your impressions with the rest of the class.

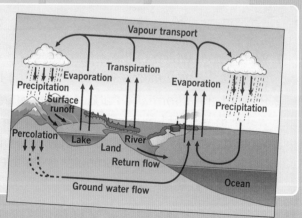

Review

Different media have different tools for getting information across. How we present information affects whether it will get across to the audience or not. Everyone has their own preferred way of receiving information because we all have different learning styles: some people prefer texts, while others favour more visual methods.

As a class, discuss the different ways of getting information across. Carry out a survey to find out which strategies members of the class prefer. Do most people like a combination of strategies?

Homework

Either:

Find out about the nitrogen cycle and present your findings using a combination of words, diagrams, charts or graphs.

Or:

Translate one of the processes in this diagram into words.

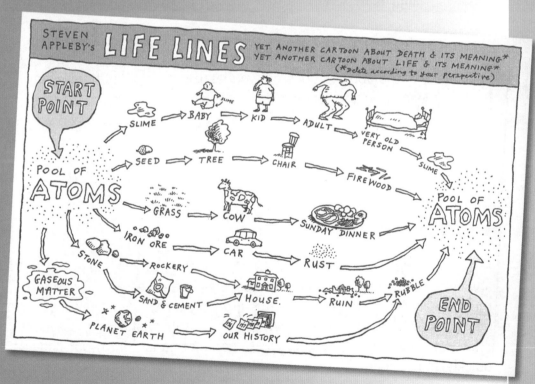

Noting what the media has to say

Aims

- To make brief, clearly organised notes of key points for later use.

Starter session

Write down the following words and phrases as quickly as you can using **abbreviations** and see if you can finish before anyone else in the class.

| and | approximately | therefore | How are you? | later |

| greater than | equals | because | Are you OK? |

How many of the abbreviations did you learn in school and how many have you learned whilst sending text messages?

As a class, discuss any abbreviations that you use in school that you find particularly useful. You could make a collection of these and display them in your classroom.

Introduction

A recent newspaper story featured a complaint by an examiner that some students were using 'text message' spellings in their essays. Using text message abbreviations in an exam is probably a bad idea (unless you are quoting a text message in a story), but using abbreviations in lessons is often a good idea, as they help you to get information onto your page as quickly as possible.

Abbreviation is the shortening of a word or phrase. Some abbreviations replace a letter or letters with an apostrophe (e.g. 'can't' for 'cannot'), while others reduce whole words to a string of letters (e.g. 'NATO' for 'North Atlantic Treaty Organisation') and others substitute symbols for whole words (e.g. '@' for 'at', '&' for 'and').

In school and in general life a great deal of information is conveyed by word of mouth; in news bulletins, in lectures, in meetings, on telephone helplines and in many other situations. Often the information you listen to is very important, and so the ability to make notes when someone is speaking – which we will be practising in this unit – is a very useful skill.

Development

A **SPEAKING AND LISTENING** READING **WRITING**

1 Below are transcripts from two radio programmes. Working as a pair, one of you reads out the transcript, at a normal speed, while the other notes down the key points.

TRANSCRIPT A

Confucius told his disciple Tsze-kung that three things are needed for government: weapons, food and trust. If a ruler can't hold on to all three, he should give up the weapons first and the food next. Trust should be guarded to the end: 'without trust we cannot stand'. Confucius' thought still convinces. Weapons did not help the Taliban when their foot soldiers lost trust and deserted. Food shortages need not topple governments when they and their rationing systems are trusted, as we know from World War II.

It isn't only rulers and governments who prize and need trust. Each of us and every profession and every institution needs trust. We need it because we have to be able to rely on others acting as they say that they will, and because we need others to accept that we will act as we say we will. The sociologist Niklas Luhmann was right that a complete absence of trust would prevent [one] even getting up in the morning.

Now swap roles.

TRANSCRIPT B

Announcer: What was your favourite part of school? Recess by any chance? Are you surprised to learn that many schoolchildren today have never heard of recess? And never had the experience? School districts across the country are eliminating or significantly reducing recess time. Rhonda Clements, president of the American Association for the Child's Right to Play, says that as many as 40 per cent of the country's school districts are now considering cutting or modifying this daily opportunity for children's unstructured play. Is this a problem? When schools are under the gun to raise academic standards, is recess really all that necessary? Well, child development experts say yes: kids need chances to bust out of the structure. They need breaks! Deanna Overton is the mother of a first grader at Wayne Elementary School in Allerton, Iowa. In previous years the school day used to include three outdoor play periods: morning, after lunch and in the afternoon. Now, however, her son's only recess comes at 1 p.m. when his day is three-quarters over. He complains to his mom.

Overton: And he will say to me, 'Mom, it's too long, I get tired, I need to get up, Mom, I need to go outside or go to the gym.' He says, 'I can't sit there that long. I'm really tired. It gets very boring to me.'

B ## SPEAKING AND LISTENING READING WRITING

With your partner, look at the notes you made and decide whether either of you missed out any vital points. Also consider the following questions.

1 Did you use abbreviations?

2 Did you use layout to separate different points?

3 Did you write in full sentences or in note form? If you wrote in note form, which parts of the sentences did you miss out?

4 Did the way that the transcripts were organised help you to make your notes?

Be prepared to report your findings to the rest of the class.

1 Using your notes only – not the passage from the book – write a paragraph on either the importance of trust or the disappearance of recesses in American schools. Be sure to write in full sentences.

2 Compare your paragraph with the original. Have you missed anything out?

Review

You have just completed a difficult but very useful task. With a partner, talk about what you found most difficult. Can you suggest good ways round some of these problems? Share your ideas with the class.

Homework

You can improve your live note-taking skills with practice. Choose one of the following tasks to complete at home.

- Make notes on the main news stories from the early evening television news. (easy)
- Make notes on the main points of a documentary on television or radio. (quite difficult)
- Make notes on the main topics of a lively discussion programme. (very difficult)

When you have completed your chosen task present your notes to your class the next day. Do not read out your notes, but try to recreate for your listeners a sense of the conversation, programme or news bulletin that they missed.

Using the Internet for research

Aims

- To look at different sources of information and decide if they are reliable.
- To learn how to acknowledge your sources of information.

Starter session

If you wanted to find out about space exploration there are a number of possible sources of information. Place the following sources in order of reliability:

- the official NASA website
- your friend who watches *Star Wars* and other similar films
- a website posted by a single enthusiast
- the *Encyclopaedia Britannica*
- a postcard with a picture of *Apollo 11* on it and a very full caption on the back
- a recently published book on the subject
- an adult who remembers watching the moon landings.

Introduction

Before the development of the Internet, if you wanted to research something seriously you had to make sure you chose a library with a good supply of relevant books. The Internet has changed all that by providing access to hundreds of thousands of individual websites. But having so much information available can cause problems as well as solving them. It can be hard to find exactly what you need, and because anyone can build a website, the quality of the information on offer can vary.

Development

SPEAKING AND LISTENING ~~READING~~ ~~WRITING~~

1 Which of the following best describes how you use the Internet?
- I only go to sites that I am told to go to by my teacher.
- I use a search engine like *Google* to find sites.
- I use a compiled search site like *Ask Jeeves* to find sites.
- I try to find sites of organisations I know about, like the RSPCA or the BBC, and to use the links they suggest.
- I don't use the Internet.

2 With a partner, discuss the advantages of these different approaches. What is your favourite strategy for finding reliable information? Report your ideas back to the class.

~~SPEAKING AND LISTENING~~ **READING** **WRITING**

Once you have typed in a search you will often have thousands of results to choose from.

1 If you were faced with the following search results on volcanoes, which would you click on first?

MTU **Volcanoes** Page
Welcome to the Michigan Technological University **Volcanoes** Page. Sponsored by the Keweenaw Volcano Observatory.

Volcanoes Online – Your Ultimate Guide to **Volcanoes** on the Net
Volcanoes Online – Your Ultimate Guide to **Volcanoes** on the Net!
Brought to you by Thinkquest Team ...

US Geological Survey, Volcano Hazards Program
... 2003 Cities on **Volcanoes** 3 Meeting in Hilo, Hawaii; 14–18 July 2003. Copyrighted painting of Pele, Hawaiian Volcano Goddess, by Herb Kane Cities on **Volcanoes** 3 ...

Volcanoes
This interactive exhibit, part of the Exhibits Collection, explores why volcanic eruptions occur. Activities in the exhibit invite visitors to melt rocks ...

How **Volcanoes** Work
... A comprehensive educational resource on the science behind **volcanoes** and volcanic processes. Description: Comprehensive educational resource on the science of volcanic processes. Topics include eruption dynamics ...

2 Write down the reasons for your choice and say why you did not choose at least one other site.

1 Which of the following two sites do you think would be the most reliable?

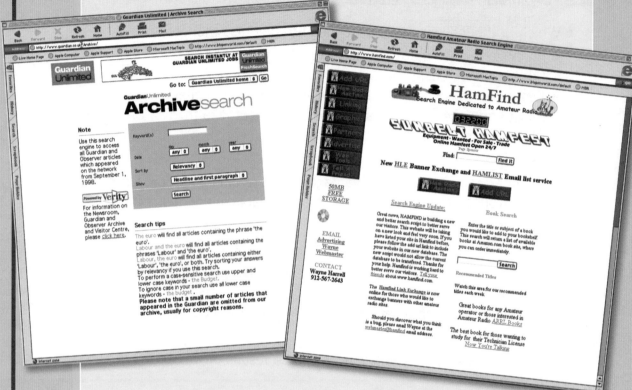

2 What aspects of these pages make you trust or distrust the site?

3 What do icons from respectable organisations such as NGfL or *The Guardian* tell us about a website?

 **Guardian** Unlimited   NGfL | National Grid for Learning

D **SPEAKING AND LISTENING** ~~READING~~ ~~WRITING~~

1 When you have found a good site with good information what do you do next? Do you:

● print out the relevant pages and stick them in your book?
● read the pages carefully and write out your own version without saying where you got the information?

- select the relevant parts of the pages, copy them into a word processor and pretend that you wrote them?
- select the relevant parts, copy them into your work and give a clear indication of where the information came from?
- do all of these things depending on the task?

2 With your partner, discuss which of these strategies you use and what is good or bad about them.

It is just as important to show the source of your information as it is to show how you worked out a problem in Maths.

3 Which of the following methods are appropriate ways of showing the source of your information?

- Writing 'I found this information on a website'.
- Copying the information and hoping the teacher thinks it's your own work.
- Using the exact URL or web address to show your source, as in http://www.bbc.co.uk/radio4/sceptred_isle/page/146.shtml?question=146
- Saying something like, 'According to the official NASA website (http://www.nasa.gov/) ... .'
- Quoting the author of the website by name.

4 Discuss each of these strategies with a partner and be prepared to feed back on them to the rest of the class.

Review

The main parts of research on the Internet are:
- finding a site
- judging whether the site is appropriate and reliable
- finding the relevant information
- acknowledging the sources of your information.

As a class, discuss which of these three tasks is the most difficult and which is the most important.

Homework
Write a brief guide for Year 7 students called 'How to use the Internet for research'.

Do 17-year-olds read J17?

Aims

- To look at how media texts are tailored to suit their audiences.
- To look at how audience responses vary.

Starter session

Match the following readers to the magazines they might read.

Boy aged 12	*Smash Hits*
Girl aged 10	*Blush!*
Boy aged 16	*Good Housekeeping*
Girl aged 16	*Loaded*
Man aged 25	*Total Football*
Woman aged 45	*Bliss*

Compare your results with the rest of the class. What do your assumptions about who reads which magazine show about the way magazines are aimed at different audiences?

Introduction

Producing and selling magazines is big business. Over a million copies of *Take a Break* are currently sold each week and over half million people buy *FHM* each month. However, if you walk into any newsagent's you will see that there is a great deal of competition in the magazine market. Most magazines succeed by targeting and keeping a particular part of the magazine-buying audience. In this unit we will be looking at how magazines aim themselves at particular audiences.

Development

Look closely at the magazine cover below and then answer the questions.

1 List the topics that are featured in this edition.

2 What do these topics have in common?

3 What does the picture suggest about the age of the girls that might read the magazine?

4 Does £1.75 seem to be expensive for girls of this age group?

5 How many of the featured topics seem to be about boys?

6 This edition of the magazine came with a free gift of some lip gloss. Why do you think this was included?

7 Why do you think this magazine uses a smaller format than most similar magazines?

8 What does the title of the magazine suggest?

Now look closely at this cover.

9 List the topics that are featured in this edition.

10 What do these topics have in common?

11 What does the picture suggest about the age of the girls that might read the magazine?

12 Does £1.75 seem to be expensive for girls of this age group? Why do you think this edition has been re-priced to 50p?

13 How many of the featured topics seem to be about boys?

14 What does the choice of a mini-book as a free gift tell you about the audience for this magazine?

15 What does the title of this magazine suggest?

16 What does the typeface used for the title suggest to you?

1 In pairs, talk about the differences between the two magazines.

2 Write a brief description of the audiences they seem to be aimed at.

We now have some fairly clear ideas about *Bliss* and *Blush!* magazines without even looking inside. We can understand more about their audiences by comparing similar sections.

"I can't wait 'til I hit the dancefloor!"
Top, £9.99, H&M
Belt, £8, Tammy
Skirt, £17, MKOne
Boots, £69.99, Shelley's
Shell bag, £12.99, Trimit
Earrings, £6, Freedom
Belt, £18, Oasis

140 bliss

LEANNE: Kiss T-shirt, £10, MK One; denim glitter skirt, £14.99, 915 at New Look; sequin bag, £25, Fine

1 What message does the reader get from the fact that the *Bliss* photo shoot took place on an exotic island whereas the *Blush!* photo is studio based?

2 What do the prices of the clothes in *Blush!* tell us about the expected spending power of its readers?

A good way of finding out about the real audience of a magazine is to look at the parts of it that the readers contribute. Both magazines have a 'Your stories' section.

In *Bliss*:
- 15-year-old Natasha tells of being beaten up by her boyfriend.
- 15-year-old Karen talks about going on the run with her boyfriend.
- 18-year-old Gretta describes how her ex tried to kill her boyfriend.
- 17-year-old Kat tells of her affair with her Maths teacher which led to him being sent to jail.

In *Blush!*:
- 11-year-old Hollie talks about dancing on stage with Kylie Minogue.
- 12-year-old Nicola tells about truanting from school.
- 13-year-old Melissa describes how being in a coma affected her attitude to life.

1 What do the ages and content of the *Bliss* readers' stories tell us about the intended audience of the magazine?

2 What do the ages and content of the *Blush!* readers' stories tell us about the intended audience of the magazine?

The age range of readers who wrote into the problem pages of *Bliss* is 12 to 18. The age range for the problem pages in *Blush!* is 10 to 13.

3 What do these facts suggest about the age of the actual audience?

Review

The title of this unit is *Do 17-year-olds read J17?* As a class, discuss whether you think the messages given out by these magazines are appropriate for their real audiences. Do you think, for instance, that both magazines appeal to readers further down the age range who want to read about what will happen next in their lives? Are there similar magazines aimed at boys?

Homework
Either:
Write two brief articles – one aimed at *Bliss* readers and one aimed at *Blush!* readers.
Or:
Write a profile for the target audience of your favourite magazine.

Pictures can't lie?

Aims

- To recognise how print and still images combine to create meaning.

Starter session

Look at the following photograph.

Write down:

- what it shows
- a caption for the picture if it was in a family album
- a caption for the picture if it was being used in a newspaper story
- the text that might go with the picture if it appeared in an advertisement.

Introduction

We tend to think of photographs as if they had a meaning all of their own, but in reality we learn to interpret pictures according to where we find them and what words or other signs go with them.

When we look at a picture on its own its meaning has to be worked out – we use the information that the picture gives to help us with this task. People who want to give their own meaning to a picture often do so by reducing the amount of information available using a process known as **cropping**. For instance, in the picture on page 32 the figures in the background and even the tank tell us something about what may be happening. If we crop the picture, these clues can be removed.

In this unit we will be investigating how the meaning of pictures can be affected by the selection of parts of an image and by the **context** in which they appear.

Development

A SPEAKING AND LISTENING **READING WRITING**

1 We can see how cropping works by looking at the photograph on the left.

Write down:
- what it shows
- what ideas you associate with this image
- the text of an advertisement that might use this image.

2 Now look at the image on the right. As you can see, the previous photo was cropped from it.
Write down:
- what you think it shows
- what ideas or feelings you think it expresses.

3 Where might you find each of the following captions if they accompanied the photograph?
- Julia was always rather dreamy.
- She'll love a carnation.
- A young woman waits to leave a single carnation at the accident site.

4 Which of the three captions above seems to you the most likely?

5 Now look at the final version of the photograph. Write down:
- what you think is happening in the photo
- whether you think it shows a 'real' or 'staged' event
- what you think the photo means.

1 With a partner, discuss:
- how the meaning of the photograph changes according to how much you see of it
- how the meaning of the photograph changes according to the caption that goes with it.

2 The photograph was taken on a peace march in Washington DC in 1967. Does knowing this fact change how you view the photograph? Do your own views about marching for peace or the necessity of war affect how you view the photograph?

Review

In this unit you have seen how photographs can be manipulated to change their meaning. Modern technology means that there are now even more ways of manipulating photographs. With a partner, discuss some of the following issues.

- Do you usually trust photographic evidence?
- When do we need to trust it?
- How do we know if pictures in newspapers are heavily cropped or not?
- Can you usually tell if an image has been altered? How?
- Does it matter if images in advertisements are digitally enhanced?
- Have you ever edited any of your own photographs?
- Do you always read the captions that go with news photographs? How might they affect your response?

Be prepared to report your discussion back to the class.

Homework

Find a photograph in a magazine and paste it into your exercise book. Write three different captions for the photo if it were to appear in:

- a family album
- a newspaper report
- an advertisement.

Suggest how the impact and meaning of the photograph could be altered by cropping it.

Write a profile for the target audience of your favourite magazine.

Leaflets and brochures

Aims

- To look at the way writers of non-fiction achieve their intentions through their use of language and the organisation of their materials.

Starter session

Dolly · Bob · Spike · Baby

With a partner, discuss the following questions.

- Which of the four dogs above do you find most charming?
- Which do you dislike the most?

Write a caption for each picture.

Introduction

Writers of persuasive non-fiction texts use a range of techniques to arouse the desired response in their audience. They use both words and images in a certain way to appeal to their readers. In this unit we will be looking at the controversial issue of vivisection and at the methods used by anti-vivisection campaigners.

Development

Look at the cover of this leaflet from the National Anti-Vivisection Society (NAVS).

1 Why do you think the brochure has a photograph of a beagle on the cover? Would a rat have been just as appropriate?

2 Why do you think the producers of the leaflet have chosen 'Animal Experiments – The Facts' as their title? What attitude does this show? Who might have been put off by a more **emotive** title such as 'Don't let him suffer'?

> ### KEY TERM
>
> **Emotive** language is language that is aimed at stirring our emotions, as opposed to 'scientific' or 'objective' language.

Here is the text from the beginning of the leaflet. Read it carefully and then answer the questions that follow.

THE FACTS

Many people believe that testing certain products on animals is cruel and unscientific, but are unsure about experiments labelled 'medical research'. This is understandable, for we all want to see medical progress.

But are experiments on animals really necessary for progress?

Is vivisection really a 'necessary evil'?

Based upon research through the scientific literature, we at the National Anti-Vivisection Society (NAVS) think not. We believe that animal experiments cannot be scientifically or morally justified. In fact, our research indicates that not only are animal experiments misleading, they can actually hold up medical progress.

The fundamental problem of animal-based research is 'species differences'. This phrase describes how species respond differently to various substances, causing problems when animal researchers try to apply animal test results to people.

Further difficulties are that distress caused to animals purely by being in the laboratory can affect the outcome of the experiment: test results can be affected by the animal's age, diet, sex, even its bedding material; results from the same test on the same species can vary from laboratory to laboratory; and artificial, laboratory-induced disease is also different from natural disease.

1 Why do you think this text is accompanied by the pictures of the monkeys in cages?

2 The language used in the leaflet is very scientific. Why do you think this is?

3 What sort of people is the leaflet trying to persuade?

4 Why do you think the writer uses the word 'we' when he says 'we all want to see medical progress'? How might this affect our response to a writer who is suggesting banning something scientists say they want?

5 Why is the question 'Is vivisection really a necessary evil?' on a line of its own?

6 Why do you think the writer tells us that the information in the leaflet is 'Based upon research through the scientific literature'? Can you find any other evidence of this approach?

The rest of the leaflet is divided into the following sections:

● Species Difference – gives examples of how different drugs affect different animals.

● Progress Without Animals – gives examples of how scientific advances have been made without animal testing.

● Confusion and Disaster – gives examples of problems caused by testing on animals.

● The Way Forward – talks about how scientific progress can be made without animal testing.

7 Can you describe how the argument is structured?

8 How would you describe this approach, emotive or scientific?

The final words in the leaflet are on a page of their own.

9 What kind of language is this?

10 What is the effect of the layout of this section?

11 Why do you think that the writers of the leaflet have chosen to end it in this way?

MILLIONS
OF ANIMALS
HOWL
SCREAM
WHINE
WHIMPER
CRY
SCREECH
SHRIEK
SQUEAL
YELP
WAIL
IN BRITISH
LABS

C SPEAKING AND LISTENING   READING   WRITING

This leaflet seems to be operating on two levels. One is mostly scientific and the other is mostly emotive. Discuss the following questions with a partner.

1 Which part of the leaflet is emotional?

2 Which part is 'objective' and scientific?

3 Why do you think the producers of the leaflet have chosen this dual approach?

4 Who do you think this leaflet is most likely to persuade – people who believe scientific research is important or people who are sympathetic to animals?

5 Would a more emotive approach in the language have improved this leaflet?

Review

The art of persuasion requires knowledge of the audience and its ideas. As a class, discuss what kind of audience this leaflet was aimed at. Which of the techniques used was most successful?

Homework

Using some of the techniques you have looked at in this unit, design a leaflet to persuade people to give up smoking.

Film reviews

Aims

- To look at how to give a considered response to a film.
- To look at how characters and events affect our response to a film.

Starter session

Below is a list of words that could be used to describe a film:

- funny
- great special effects
- excellent performances
- well-structured
- spine-tingling
- moving
- action-packed
- breathtaking
- family entertainment.

Write each word into a column headed either 'nouns and noun phrases' or 'adjectives and adjectival phrases'.

Introduction

Reviews of any kind have two major functions:

- to help someone who has not experienced something to decide whether to try it
- to record the reaction of a viewer, listener or reader to a particular experience.

A third function is to let the producers of a media text know how well they have done. In this unit, we will investigate some film reviews and think about how to write them.

Development

Here are two reviews of the film *Shrek*. Read them carefully and then answer the questions that follow.

SHREK – REVIEWED BY ANNE DONNELLY

A terrifying ogre, a wicked prince, a chatterbox donkey, a beautiful princess – put them together and what do you get? Shrek!

Shrek is a hilarious movie and a great example of sophisticated film-making now, in the 21st century.

Set in a fairytale land, Shrek is a tale of love, courage and what to do if your backyard gets inhabited by hundreds of fairytale characters. Shrek, a lime green ogre, sets out to rescue a princess for the wicked ruler of the land, who promises to rid his backyard of all the storyboard heroes that are hiding there. It is also interesting to see how Shrek's character develops as he changes from a lonely, selfish, unhappy and hideous ogre to a friendly, generous, joyful and hideous ogre. His main friend throughout is the donkey, sticking by Shrek and cracking jokes left and right.

Shrek is an excellent film, so well made that at times I believed the animated characters were real! It is hilarious and has a great storyline. With all these good points and an unexpected twist, Shrek will appeal to audiences young and old.

I give it 5/5.

Anne Donnelly, aged 12, is the winner of a British Film Institute review competition.

1 How much of this review is a record of the reviewer's reaction?

2 How much is information about the film itself?

3 Would you say that the review focused mostly on characters or events?

4 Do you think this review would make you want to go and see *Shrek* if you hadn't seen it?

5 Choose a sentence from this review and explain why you like it.

6 Why do you think Anne Donnelly has provided a score at the end? Who is this helpful to?

7 Who do you think is the target audience for this review?

There'll be bluebirds, ogres…

Shrek (90 mins, U)

Directed by Andrew Adamson and Vicki Jenson; featuring the voices of Eddie Murphy, Mike Myers, Cameron Diaz

The computer-animated film *Shrek*, the joint directorial debut of Andrew Adamson and Vicky Jenson, is, I believe, the first of Steig's[1] 20 children's books to reach the screen and in its properly modest fashion seems to me family entertainment of the highest order. It is, however, in its smooth, sculptured style visually far removed from Steig's own idiosyncratic line. Like the Rob Reiner–William Goldman live-action fable *The Princess Bride*, *Shrek* is a fairy story about fairy stories and it begins disarmingly with a bland tale being read from the turning pages of a traditional children's book. This is deliberately misleading, because the book is being read in the strong Scottish accent (provided by Mike Myers) of a hideous, green-faced ogre who is using the book as lavatory paper in his outdoor privy and mocking its contents. This ogre is called Shrek, which is roughly German for shock and horror, and is the name of the hideous-looking actor Max Schreck, who played Dracula in Murnau's *Nosferatu*,[2] a film to which this one centrally refers.

The ogre, who begins the day bathing in mud and uses the wax from his ears as candles, lives alone in a hideous swamp, believing himself to horrify and be abhorred by other men. Suddenly, creatures from fairy tales arrive in his domain – the three blind mice, Snow White and the seven dwarfs, Pinocchio and so on – exiled there by Lord Farquaad (John Lithgow). The dreadful Farquaad wants to rule a conformist city of obsequious citizens who behave according to TV-style studio cards telling them to 'Applaud', 'Laugh' or maintain 'Revered Silence'.

Attaching himself to the ogre as a very reluctant companion–assistant is a talking donkey, a real wise-ass amusingly voiced by Eddie Murphy, who accompanies Shrek on a quest to win the hand of the beautiful Princess Fiona (Cameron Diaz) for Farquaad. The tyrant needs her, for only by marrying a true princess can he proclaim himself king. The vainglorious Farquaad is too cowardly to undertake the mission to Fiona's Piranesi-like[3] castle himself because she's protected by a ferocious, fire-eating dragon.

Needless to say, Shrek and the Donkey succeed, but then comes the homeward journey with their beautiful prize and the turning of the tables on the wretched Farquaad. There are here, of course, parodic elements of Cyrano de Bergerac[4] in Shrek's courtship of Fiona and his inevitable love for her.

Naturally, they quarrel endlessly, but in several respects they strike it off well, because she has a sharp tongue, some skills in karate, which serve to repel Robin Hood's rapacious band, and when the ogre inflates a toad into a floating balloon she does the same with a snake. But she also has an unusual characteristic, the result of some sort of spell, which makes her like Dracula, a victim of the change between night and day, and produces a twist on the fairy-tale convention. Her heart is true, but her beauty is skin-deep.

The movie is a constant delight for its exuberant simplicity, its avoidance of sensational effects, its wit and a true feeling that transcends sentimentality. Except for a single scene, it avoids the usual animated movie songs by the likes of Elton John and Tim Rice and, indeed, makes jokes about the awful voices of Fiona, whose high notes make a friendly bluebird explode, and the Donkey, who is only allowed to hum.

And the picture concludes with an ensemble version of the Monkees' 'I'm a Believer', a tribute to four untalented musicians.

---

1 William Steig is the author of the original book version of *Shrek*.
2 *Nosferatu* is a famous vampire movie, made in 1922.
3 Piranesi was an Italian graphic artist, famous for engravings and etchings.
4 Cyrano de Bergerac is a character from a play set in France in 1640.
   He has an incredibly large nose, but is very witty, and woos the lovely Roxanne on behalf of his friend Christian.

Philip French, the author of this review, has been *The Observer* film critic since 1978.

8 How much of this review is a record of the reviewer's reaction?

9 How much is information about the film itself?

10 Would you say that the review focused mostly on characters or events?

11 What moral has Philip French drawn from this film?

12 Do you think this review would make you want to go and see *Shrek* if you hadn't seen it?

13 Why do you think Philip French has included so much information about the author and where the name Shrek comes from?

14 Who do you think is the target audience for this review?

B SPEAKING AND LISTENING   READING   WRITING

With a partner, discuss both reviews.

1 Which review gives you a better sense of the film?

2 How would these reviews have been different if Shrek had been a live-action film or a stage play?

3 As a pair, write some advice, based on these two reviews, on what should be included in a film review.

Be prepared to report your ideas back to the class.

Review

As a class, share your opinions about film reviews. Do you read them to help you decide to go and see a film? Do you avoid them so that you don't find out about the story of the film? Do you read them after you've seen a film, to see what other people thought? What is your idea of a good film review?

Homework

Follow your own advice and write a review of a film you have seen recently.

Year 7 SATs

Chapter 1

Harvey, Half-Devoured

The great grey beast February had eaten Harvey Swick alive. Here he was, buried in the belly of that smothering month, wondering if he would ever find his way out through the cold coils that lay between here and Easter.

He didn't think much of his chances. More than likely he'd become so bored as the hours crawled by that one day he'd simply forget to breathe. Then maybe people would wonder why such a fine young lad had perished in his prime. It would become a celebrated mystery, which wouldn't be solved until some great detective decided to recreate a day in Harvey's life.

Then, and only then, would the grim truth be discovered. The detective would first follow Harvey's route to school every morning, trekking through the dismal streets. Then he'd sit at Harvey's desk, and listen to the pitiful drone of the history teacher and the science teacher, and wonder how the heroic boy had managed to keep his eyes open. And finally, as the wasted day dwindled to dusk, he'd trace the homeward trek, and as he set foot on the step from which he had departed that morning, and people asked him – as they would – why such a sweet soul as Harvey had died, he would shake his head and say:

'It's very simple.'

'Oh?' the curious crowd would say. 'Do tell.'

And, brushing away a tear, the detective would reply:

'Harvey Swick was eaten by the great grey beast February.'

IT WAS A monstrous month, that was for sure; a dire and dreary month. The pleasures of Christmas, both sharp and sweet, were already dimming in Harvey's memory, and the promise of summer was so remote as to be mythical. There'd be a spring break, of course, but how far off was that? Five weeks? Six? Mathematics wasn't his strong point, so he didn't irritate himself further by attempting – and failing – to calculate the days. He simply knew that long before the sun came to save him he would have withered away in the belly of the beast.

SAD Information sheet

- Home Page

INFORMATION
- SAD
- Sleep
- Jetlag
- Alzheimer's Sundowning
- Site Search

PRODUCTS
- Light Therapy Devices
- Bodyclocks™
- Jet Lag Combat Kit
- Window Light
- Solon

- Order Forms

CONTACT
- Send us Email
- Forum
- Contact

Please help a student do some research into SAD by completing this anonymous questionnaire

If you want to know more, please, just get in touch

SAD

Seasonal Affective Disorder
Winter Depression
The Winter Blues

What is SAD?

SAD stands for Seasonal Affective Disorder.

Animals react to the changing season with changes in mood and behaviour and human beings are no exception. Most people find they eat and sleep slightly more in winter and dislike the dark mornings and short days. For some, however, symptoms are severe enough to disrupt their lives and to cause considerable distress. These people are suffering from SAD.

How does it affect people?

Sufferers have to endure most of the following:
Sleep Problems – oversleeping but not refreshed, cannot out of bed, needing a nap in the afternoon
Overeating – carbohydrate craving leading to overweight
Depression – despair, misery, guilt, anxiety, normal tasks become frustratingly difficult, hopelessness
Family problems – avoiding company, irritability, loss of libido, loss of feeling
Lethargy – too tired to cope, everything an effort
Physical Symptoms – often joint pain or stomach problems, lowered resistance to infection
Behavioural problems – especially in young people

The symptoms tend to start from around September each year, lasting until April but are at their worst in the darkest months.

Who does it affect?

The standard figure says that around 2% of people in Northern Europe suffer badly, with many more (10%) putting up with milder symptoms (sub-syndromal SAD or the winter blues). Across the world the incidence increases with distance from the equator, except where there is snow on the ground when it becomes less common. More women than men are diagnosed as having SAD. Children and adolescents are also vulnerable.

What causes it?

The problem stems from the lack of bright light in winter. Researchers have proved that bright light makes a difference to the brain chemistry, although the exact means by which sufferers are affected is not yet known. It is not a psychosomatic or imaginary illness.

More about the mechanisms and what happens

What treatment is there?

As the cause is lack of bright light, the treatment is to be in bright light every day by using a light box or a similar bright light therapy device. (Going to a brightly-lit climate, whether skiing or somewhere hot, is indeed a cure). The preferred level of light is about as bright as a spring morning on a clear day and for most people sitting in front of a light box, allowing the light to reach the eyes, for between 1/4 and 3/4 hour daily will be sufficient to alleviate the symptoms. The user does not have to stare at the light, but can watch TV or read or similar, just allowing the light to reach the eyes. Outside In have a complete range of suitable lights, all in line with the research findings from medical and academic facilities. They are all available on our pioneering HOME TRIAL system, and most of them VAT FREE for personal users.

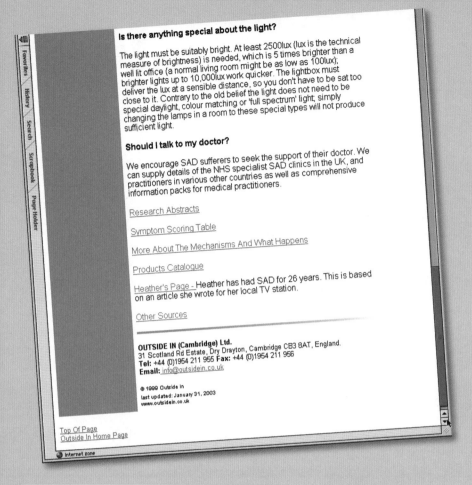

Is there anything special about the light?

The light must be suitably bright. At least 2500lux (lux is the technical measure of brightness) is needed, which is 5 times brighter than a well lit office (a normal living room might be as low as 100lux); brighter lights up to 10,000lux work quicker. The lightbox must deliver the lux at a sensible distance, so you don't have to be sat too close to it. Contrary to the old belief the light does not need to be special daylight, colour matching or 'full spectrum' light; simply changing the lamps in a room to these special types will not produce sufficient light.

Should I talk to my doctor?

We encourage SAD sufferers to seek the support of their doctor. We can supply details of the NHS specialist SAD clinics in the UK, and practitioners in various other countries as well as comprehensive information packs for medical practitioners.

Research Abstracts

Symptom Scoring Table

More About The Mechanisms And What Happens

Products Catalogue

Heather's Page - Heather has had SAD for 26 years. This is based on an article she wrote for her local TV station.

Other Sources

OUTSIDE IN (Cambridge) Ltd.
31 Scotland Rd Estate, Dry Drayton, Cambridge CB3 8AT, England.
Tel: +44 (0)1954 211 955 **Fax:** +44 (0)1954 211 956
Email: info@outsidein.co.uk

© 1999 Outside In
last updated: January 31, 2003
www.outsidein.co.uk

Top Of Page
Outside In Home Page

Internet zone

Year 7 Test Questions

Answer the following questions in your books.

Questions 1–4 are about *Harvey, Half-Devoured*.

1 From the first paragraph, write down the month that is causing Harvey so much trouble. *(1 mark)*

2 In the first paragraph, what is the month being compared to? *(1 mark)*

3 In paragraphs two and three the author uses exaggeration to make the depth of Harvey's feelings clear to the reader.

   a Pick out two phrases which show this exaggeration. *(2 marks)*

   b Explain why you think this exaggeration is effective. *(1 mark)*

4 In the whole text, how does the writer make Harvey's feelings clear?
You should comment on how the writer:
- sets the scene
- introduces Harvey's character
- shows how hopeless he feels.

(5 marks)

Questions 5–9 are about the SAD Information Sheet web page.

5 From paragraph 2, give two of the ways that Seasonal Affective Disorder (SAD) affects people.

(2 marks)

6 Why do you think the sub-headings on this web page are written as questions? Suggest one reason.

(1 mark)

7 From sections 5 and 6, sum up the method of treatment recommended by Outside In.

(2 marks)

8 In the whole web page, explain how the writer presents scientific information as a way of advertising a product.

(5 marks)

9 Explain one way in which the first paragraph is effective as an introduction to this web page.
Support your answer with a quotation.

(2 marks)

Question 10 is about *Harvey, Half-Devoured* and SAD Information Sheet web page.

10 The *Harvey, Half-Devoured* and the SAD Information Sheet are very different texts.
Copy out and complete the table below, suggesting:
- one purpose of each text
- one word or phrase to describe the language used in each text.

	Harvey, Half-Devoured	*SAD Information Sheet*
Purpose of text		
Language used in the text		

(2 marks)

Researching Dickens

Aims

- To use different strategies when doing your own research.
- To use your knowledge of how texts and ICT databases are organised.
- To learn how to acknowledge sources.

Starter session

The letters of the following anagrams have been placed in alphabetical order. Work out what each word is and then write down the list in alphabetical order. (Clue: they're all types of food.)

aaabnn	aegnor	aelpp	aegpr
firtu	abeeegltv	aooptt	acorrt

Introduction

This unit is about research. Successful research depends on your understanding of how knowledge is organised.

Match the following methods of organisation to the research resource.

alphabetical order by author

words in alphabetical order

information in 'fields'

Dewey Decimal Classification system

topics in alphabetical order

Universal Resource Locator (URL)

computer database

encyclopaedia

page on the Internet

fiction section in a library

dictionary

non-fiction section of a library

Development

Look at these pieces of information about Dickens, taken from different sources.

Dictionary

Dickens /dɪk-ɪnz/
Charles (John Huffam), pen name Boz. 1812–70, English novelist, famous for the humour and sympathy of his characterisation and his criticism of social injustice. His major works include *The Pickwick Papers* (1837), *Oliver Twist* (1839), *Nicholas Nickleby* (1839), *Old Curiosity Shop* (1840-41), *Martin Chuzzlewit* (1844), *David Copperfield* (1850), *Bleak House* (1853), *Little Dorrit* (1857) and *Great Expectations* (1861).

Website

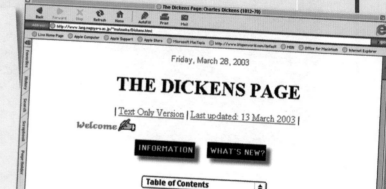

Friday, March 28, 2003

THE DICKENS PAGE

| Text Only Version | Last updated: 13 March 2003 |

Welcome

INFORMATION   WHAT'S NEW?

Table of Contents

"Wery glad to see you, indeed, and hope our acquaintance may be a long 'un, as the gen'I'm'n said to the fi' pun' note." (Sam Weller)

E-texts Recommended	Project Gutenberg Concordance	Bibliomania Filmography	Great Books Life of Dickens	MasterTexts Discussion Board

| Life and Works | Japan Dickens Fellowship | Carol Discussion Board |

CD-Rom encyclopaedia

Charles Dickens

◄◄◄ BACK   NEXT ►►►

INTRODUCTION Dickens, Charles John Huffam (1812-1870), English novelist and one of the most popular writers in the history of literature. His ability to combine comedy, pathos, and social satire in his serialized novels won him thousands of contemporary readers, and many of his characters, such as Mr Micawber, Mrs Gamp, Mr Pickwick, Quilp, and Uriah Heep, have entered the British national consciousness.

II EARLY LIFE Dickens was born near Portsmouth: his father was a clerk in the Navy Pay Office. The happiest period of Dickens's troubled childhood was spent in Chatham, although the family moved around a great deal. By early 1824, the family was in financial trouble and the 12-year old Dickens was sent to work for a few months at a shoe-polish warehouse on the banks of the Thames. A few days later, his father was arrested for debt. Dickens recalled this painful experience in the early chapters of *David Copperfield* (1849-1850), and it seemed to haunt him all his life: he called it "the secret agony of my soul". His father was imprisoned in the Marshalsea Prison and, except for Charles, who had lodgings in Camden, and his sister, who was studying music, all the family lived in the prison with him like the Dorrit family in the first part of *Little Dorrit* (1855-1857). In the summer of 1824, after Dickens's father's case was heard by the Insolvency Court, the family was allowed to leave the prison but Dickens continued to work in the warehouse until 1825, when his father sent him to school at Wellington House Academy.

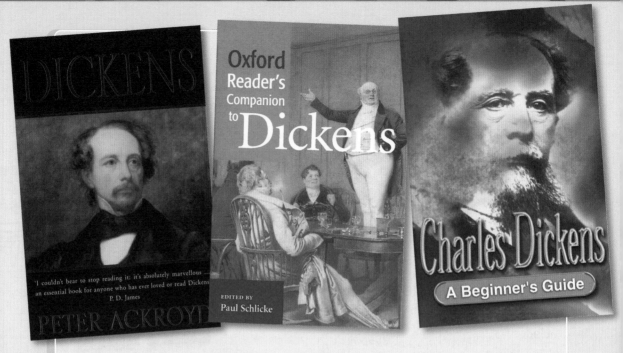

Answer the following questions in your books.

1 What is the advantage of looking Dickens up in a dictionary rather than an encyclopaedia?

2 What are the advantages of a CD-Rom-based encyclopaedia over a paper-based one? What are the disadvantages?

3 Why might you have more faith in a CD-Rom or paper-based encyclopaedia than in information from a website?

4 Why does the Dickens website offer a text only version?

5 The URL for the Dickens website contains the letters 'ac.jp'.
   ● Where in the world is the site located?
   ● What does the 'ac' part mean?
   ● How does the 'ac' part affect your attitude to the information on the site?

6 If you were using this web page, which hyperlink would you follow first? Explain your choice.

7 Would the three books on Dickens be on the same shelf in a library that used the Dewey Decimal system? (You might have to ask a librarian for help on this question if your school does not use the Dewey Decimal system.)

8 Which of the three books would be most useful if you wanted to know about the following:
   ● the circumstances under which Dickens wrote his books
   ● interpretations of some of Dickens' works
   ● general information on Dickens' writing?

9 If you were trying to find out about Dickens' character Fagin, which of the three books would you go to first?

10 Which of the sources of information shown here do you think will contain the most information on Dickens himself?

B SPEAKING AND LISTENING **READING** **WRITING**

Good research is always checkable; that is, your readers should always be able to go back to the source of your information. There are two main ways of acknowledging your sources – as you go along or through a **bibliography**.

KEY TERM

A **bibliography** is, strictly speaking, a list of books, but might also contain web addresses, newspaper references, CD-Rom titles, etc. Ideally, a bibliography should contain:

- the name of the author
- the title of the source
- the publisher's name if the source is printed or on CD-Rom
- the web address if the source is on the Internet
- the date of publication or last update.

Here are some ways of acknowledging sources. Match them to the resources in this unit.

Dickens by Peter Ackroyd, Mandarin, 1991
Microsoft Encarta Encyclopedia, Microsoft Corporation, 2002
Collins English Dictionary, HarperCollins, 1995
http://www.lang.nagoya-u.ac.jp/~matsuoka/Dickens.html, 2002

Review

As a class, discuss the advantages and disadvantages of ICT-based research (i.e. the Internet and CD-Roms) and paper-based methods.

Homework

Write a brief report on the life and works of William Shakespeare, using more than one source of information. Make sure that you acknowledge your sources.

Soap opera notes

Aims

- To make notes in different ways.
- To choose a note form which suits the purpose.
- To abbreviate for speed and ease of retrieval.

Starter session

Write down the following in full.
- I wil hav 2 C U l8r. I havnt gt ☺2 C U now. My bus wil b here in < 1 min.
- $C=2\pi r$
- UEFA OKs MAN U BID

Introduction

Getting things down on paper (or on screen) is a time-consuming business. In this unit we will be looking at how we can note down information as quickly and efficiently as possible, using abbreviations and other strategies.

Development

A SPEAKING AND LISTENING READING **WRITING**

An important principle of note-taking is to understand how a text works.

1 Where would you expect the most important piece of information in a paragraph to be?

2 What is the function of headings in an information text?

Read this extract from a newspaper article and answer the questions that follow.

THE MAGNIFICENT SEVEN RIDE AGAIN (AND AGAIN ...)

There are no new ideas, there are only different ways of saying the same thing. Andy Medhurst pinpoints the seven basic plots that lie at the heart of all fiction. [...]

Here [...] are the Seven Pillars of Television. Call them formulaic (if you dislike the resulting programme) or archetypal (if you love it), these are the building blocks of television fiction. While a programme relying on only one of the seven runs the risk of obviousness and banality, shrewder and more satisfying series combine, reshuffle and expand on them – an episode of *Casualty* or *London's Burning* may have four or five in play at once – and to maintain credibility they also need adapting to changing cultural and social circumstances.

Romeo and Juliet

[...] Boy meets girl is literally the case in the adolescent wonderland of Australian soaps [...] *Love Hurts* was a drawn-out, bitterly mature version of this story, and *Cheers* had a comic inflection of the same in Sam's endless, if futile, pursuit of Diane. [...]

The easiest way to complicate the love narrative is to introduce a third party, and whether it's the gormless Welshman intruding on the couple upstairs in *Lipstick On Your Collar* or the Nathan/Sarah/Tug imbroglio in *Home and Away*, the structure is the same. [...]

The Spider and the Fly

The temptress ensnaring the lust-struck male is a staple of the more melodramatic soaps – most memorably incarnated, tongue-in-cheek never smudging the incandescent lipstick, by Joan Collins in Spelling's *Dynasty*. Bet Gilroy has had her web-weaving moments behind the bar of the Rovers', *EastEnders'* Bianca would clearly like to be fatally attractive when she grows up, and Patsy in *Absolutely Fabulous* enjoys a little luring between bottles of Bollie. [...]

The Fatal Flaw

The Achilles' heel that leads to the destruction of the previously impregnable individual was once the foundation of classical tragedy; on TV it's the cornerstone of crime drama, where it belongs not to the hero but to the villain. *Columbo, Spender, Miss Marple, Cracker* – all busy themselves with seeking the crack in the crook's armour. Only the tone varies, from the gravitas of *Morse* via the sour urban noir of *Between the Lines* to the whimsy of *Murder She Wrote*. The most economical use of the plot is still *Scooby Doo*.

The Faustian Bargain

The long-term debt that must be paid, the uncovered secret that eventually damns, the inescapability of fate – this plot is particularly useful for soaps, where the endlessness of the time-scale gives lots of scope for the slow-burning story. *Brookside* does this type of thing best – witness the revelation of Josh's real father, the [...] tortured guilt of murderous Barry, and the timebomb [of] the corpse buried under Mandy's patio. We long-term viewers bide our time, confident that retribution will one day materialise.

Candide

The innocent abroad, naïve optimism triumphant. You can't keep a good man down is a staple plot found more often in cinema (James Stewart in *Harvey*, Peter Sellers in *Being There*, Tom Hanks in [...] *Forrest Gump*) than television. Television comedy has, however, used it, often refracted through slapstick – Frank Spencer, Mr Bean, *Mork and Mindy's* Mork. [...]

Cinderella

Unrecognised virtue recognised at last, goodness triumphant after initial vilification, rewards achieved through transformed circumstances in its undisguised form, the Cinderella plot is a touch too sugary for today's jaded tastes, and [...] more suited to the one-off narrative of film than the repetitive structures of television, but there will always be an audience for adaptations of Cartland and Cookson. The deliciously predictable *Dr Quinn: Medicine Woman* is a comparable fable – a decorative frontier medic has cure for mystery illness, is disbelieved by head-shaking townsfolk, proves her mettle and saves both the patient and the day. *Superman*, using a phone booth as a larger, rectangular glass slipper, is a more butch Cinderella variant [...].

1 Make notes on the above extract so that you can explain its main points to another person.

2 Compare your notes with a partner's. Which features of the text helped you the most? Which of you wrote least?

C SPEAKING AND LISTENING READING WRITING

We need to use different strategies when making notes about something like an episode of a soap opera. Again, we need to use our knowledge of how soap operas work. Below are some basic facts.

- Each episode of a soap opera consists of a number of storylines.
- Some storylines will just be beginning, others will be at a crisis, and some will be winding down.
- The different storylines are intermingled and given different amounts of time.

1 Why do you think the different storylines are at different stages in any given episode?

2 With a partner, discuss your favourite soap opera and identify two or three current storylines.

A good way of making notes on a soap opera is to use a table. Remember that one character could be in more than one storyline.

Scene	1	2	3	4	5	6	7
Storyline 1	A meets B			A and B kiss			
Storyline 2		C asks D for money					
Storyline 3			E and F at pub				
Storyline 4					G and A at home		

With a partner, predict how many 'scene' columns and 'storyline' rows you would need to cover a single episode of your favourite soap. Draw up a table with the correct number of rows and columns.

E **SPEAKING AND LISTENING**   READING   **WRITING**

A different strategy again is needed if we want to explain the relationships between the characters – we can do this by using a spider diagram.

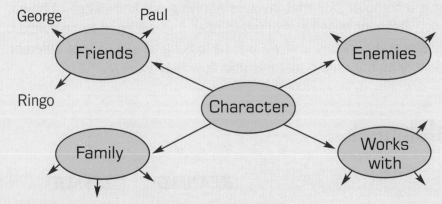

1 Fill out a spider diagram for a fictional character.
2 Discuss with a partner what mapping out a character's relationships shows about the character.

Seeing through the fog

Aims

- To use a range of reading strategies.
- To review your skills as active, critical readers.

Starter session

Identify and write down where you might read the following sentences.

- ENGLAND IN TROUBLE AGAIN.
- England provides historical monuments and picturesque views aplenty.
- The last successful conquest of England by a foreign power was in 1066.
- England. Cool, calm, collected. Try it.

Compare your answers with your partner. What clues did you use to make your decision?

Introduction

Reading is a complex skill that involves applying our knowledge of how a text works. Different texts have different rules and we need to be aware of how these operate. In this unit we will be looking at a variety of different texts, identifying their main features and how they work.

Development

A SPEAKING AND LISTENING   **READING**   **WRITING**

An important principle of note-taking is to understand how a text works.

1 Where would you expect the most important piece of information in a paragraph to be?

2 What is the function of headings in an information text?

THIS IS YOUR CAPTAIN: I DON'T KNOW HOW TO LAND THE PLANE

By Paul Marston, Transport Correspondent

PASSENGERS screamed when the pilot of a no-frills Go flight from Newcastle to Stansted airport said he did not know how to land in fog.

Some of them made panicky phone calls to relatives on their mobiles as the Boeing 737 circled for half an hour in the murk.

Karen Barichievy, from London, one of the 92 passengers, said: 'We had started to wonder if something was wrong when we hovered over Stansted for so long.

'People screamed and gasped when the pilot came over the loudspeaker saying he could not land because he was in training. They couldn't believe what they had heard. People were phoning their families. There was a real sense of fear.' The plane was diverted to East Midlands airport, where visibility was good, and the co-pilot emerged from the cockpit to explain.

Miss Barichievy, 25, a trainee reporter, said: 'He stood at the front of the cabin and apologised, admitting that this flight was part of his training and he had not yet been certificated to land in fog. He looked embarrassed.'

Regulations require both pilots on any flight to have category 3 qualifications if a low visibility landing is to be made. But only one of the two pilots on Flight GO612 last Friday held such a licence.

The airline had gambled on the weather staying clear. So when fog quickly enveloped Stansted, the co-pilot, who was flying the aircraft, had to abort.

After an hour at East Midlands, a category 3 pilot arrived in a van and was cheered and applauded. The flight, for which passengers had paid between £20 and £60, eventually reached Stansted at midnight, two and a half hours late.

Captain Ed Winter, Go's chief operating officer, said the co-pilot was new and had to complete three landings using category 3 procedures in clear weather before being allowed to execute one in reduced visibility.

He added: 'There had been no fog forecast for this flight, but unfortunately fog came into Stansted very quickly.'

TEXT **2**

FOG INDEX

How High is Your Fog Index?

1. Find the average number of words you use per sentence. Take a fair sample of 5 to 8 sentences. Count clearly independent clauses as separate sentences. Example: 'By and by I ran; I jumped; hid.' This counts as three sentences.

2. Calculate the percentage of words that are three syllables or more. Don't count proper names. Don't count verbs that make three syllables, or adding -es or -ed.

③ Add these two figures. Example: if your average number of words per sentence was 15, and the percentage of words of three syllables or more was 12%, you would add 15 and 12 to get 27.

④ Multiply that sum by 0.4. The resulting number is your Fog Index, a rough measure of how many years of schooling it would take to understand what you have written. In our example, multiplying 27 by 0.4 equals a Fog Index of 10.8. The Bible, Shakespeare, Mark Twain, and TV Guide all have Fog Indexes of about 6. Time, Newsweek, and the Wall St. Journal average about 11. If you find your Index soaring into the teens (or higher!) – beware – you've lost most of your audience in the dense fog.

CHAPTER I

In Chancery

London. Michaelmas term lately over, and the Lord Chancellor sitting in Lincoln's Inn Hall. Implacable November weather. As much mud in the streets as if the waters had but newly retired from the face of the earth, and it would not be wonderful to meet a Megalosaurus, forty feet long or so, waddling like an elephantine lizard up Holborn Hill. Smoke lowering down from chimney-pots, making a soft black drizzle, with flakes of soot in it as big as full-grown snowflakes – gone into mourning, one might imagine, for the death of the sun. Dogs, undistinguishable in mire. Horses, scarcely better; splashed to their very blinkers. Foot passengers, jostling one another's umbrellas in a general infection of ill temper, and losing their foot-hold at street-corners, where tens of thousands of other foot passengers have been slipping and sliding since the day broke (if this day ever broke), adding new deposits to the crust upon crust of mud, sticking at those points tenaciously to the pavement, and accumulating at compound interest.

Fog everywhere. Fog up the river, where it flows among green aits and meadows; fog down the river, where it rolls deified among the tiers of shipping and the waterside pollutions of a great (and dirty) city. Fog on the Essex marshes, fog on the Kentish heights. Fog creeping into the cabooses of collier-brigs; fog lying out on the yards and hovering in the rigging of great ships; fog drooping on the gunwales of barges and small boats. Fog in the eyes and throats of ancient Greenwich pensioners, wheezing by the firesides of their wards; fog in the stem and bowl of the afternoon pipe of the wrathful skipper, down in his close cabin; fog cruelly pinching the toes and fingers of his shivering little 'prentice boy on deck. Chance people on the bridges peeping over the parapets into a nether sky of fog, with fog all round them, as if they were up in a balloon and hanging in the misty clouds.

FOG ON THE TYNE

Sittin' in a sleazy snack-bar suckin' sickly sausage rolls,
Slippin' down slowly, slippin' down sideways, think I'll sign off the dole.
'Cause the fog on the Tyne is all mine, all mine
The fog on the Tyne is all mine
The fog on the Tyne is all mine, all mine,
The fog on the Tyne is all mine.

Could a copper catch a crooked coffin maker, could a copper comprehend,
That a crooked coffin maker is just an undertaker who undertakes to be a friend.
'Cause the fog on the Tyne is all mine, all mine
The fog on the Tyne is all mine
The fog on the Tyne is all mine, all mine,
The fog on the Tyne is all mine.

For each of the texts, answer the following questions.

1 What kind of text is this?

2 Where would you expect to find this text?

3 What features of the text identify it?

4 How is it structured?

5 What audience does it seem to be aimed at?

6 Why might the reader read the text?

7 How many times would you have to read the text through in order to fully understand it?

B *SPEAKING AND LISTENING* READING WRITING

With a partner, discuss the different text types you have looked at.

1 Which texts are meant to entertain?

2 Which of the four texts would you say is the most highly structured?

3 Which text type was the most difficult to identify?

4 How big a clue was layout? For instance, what if Text 1 had been set out like Text 4?

Review

Different text types require different reading skills. In small groups, review each of the texts in this unit and discuss how difficult each is to understand. Talk about why it is difficult – think about things such as content, length, organisation and format. What reading techniques can you use to help you find your way around the text? Share your ideas with the rest of the class.

Homework

Find a short text and either copy it out or paste a copy into your book. Write a brief description of the text in terms of its type, its intended audience, the features it contains and how it is organised. What strategies would you use when reading it?

Themes: Mort(ality) and Death

Aims

- To look at the development of themes, values and ideas in two texts.

Starter session

Many people feel uncomfortable talking about death, so instead of saying someone died they will use a **euphemism** – a softer term.

Here are a few examples, some respectful, some not.

gone to a better place   sleeping with the fishes   passed over

pushing up daises   went to sleep   met their maker

Write down five other euphemisms for dying.

Introduction

In the world imagined by Terry Pratchett in his story *Mort*, Death is a real figure whose job is to cut the thread of life that binds a body to its soul. People's lives are measured by a sort of hourglass; when the sand runs out, it is time for them to die. Mort is a human boy who, as Death's apprentice, has disobeyed his master by applying ideas like justice and fairness to his task. He has been aided in this by Death's adopted human daughter Ysabell.

In this unit we are going to examine two versions of the story. One is the original text-based version of the story and the other is a graphic novel adaptation.

With a partner, discuss what we mean by the idea of 'a story'. Is a story in words the same as a story in words and pictures? Report your ideas back to the class.

Development

Here is one of the final scenes from *Mort* in novel form.

'Doesn't seem very fair, does it? Don't the gods bother about justice and mercy?' snapped Ysabell. Without anyone quite noticing she had picked up the sword.

Death grinned. I APPLAUD YOUR EFFORTS, he said, BUT THEY AVAIL YOU NAUGHT. STAND ASIDE.

'No.'

YOU MUST BE AWARE THAT EVEN LOVE IS NO DEFENCE AGAINST ME. I AM SORRY.

Ysabell raised the sword. '*You're* sorry?'

STAND ASIDE, I SAY.

'No. You're just being vindictive. It's not fair!'

Death bowed his skull for a moment, then looked up with his eyes blazing.

YOU WILL DO AS YOU ARE TOLD.

'I will not.'

YOU'RE MAKING THIS VERY DIFFICULT.

'Good.'

Death's fingers drummed impatiently on the scytheblade, like a mouse tapdancing on a tin. He seemed to be thinking. He looked at Ysabell standing over Mort, and then turned and looked at the others crouching against a shelf.

NO, he said eventually. NO. I CANNOT BE BIDDEN. I CANNOT BE FORCED. I WILL DO ONLY THAT WHICH I KNOW TO BE RIGHT.

He waved a hand, and the sword whirred out of Ysabell's grasp. He made another complicated gesture and the girl herself was picked up and pressed gently but firmly against the nearest pillar.

Mort saw the dark reaper advance on him again, blade swinging back for the final stroke. He stood over the boy.

YOU DON'T KNOW HOW SORRY THIS MAKES ME, he said.

Mort pulled himself on to his elbows.

'I might,' he said.

Death gave him a surprised look for several seconds, and then started to laugh. The sound bounced eerily around the room, ringing off the shelves as Death, still laughing like an earthquake in a graveyard, held Mort's own glass in front of its owner's eyes.

Mort tried to focus. He saw the last grain of sand skid down the glossy surface, teeter on the edge and then drop, tumbling in slow motion, towards the bottom. Candlelight flickered off its tiny silica facets as it spun gently downward. It landed soundlessly, throwing up a tiny crater.

The light in Death's eyes flared until it filled Mort's vision and the sound of his laughter rattled the universe.

And then Death turned the hourglass over.

Here is the same scene in graphic novel format.

1 With a partner, compare the two versions of the story and make notes on the following:

- the role played by Ysabell
- the changes made to the dialogue
- the differences between Pratchett's descriptions and the illustrations.

Try to decide why there are differences between the two versions.

WRITING

Answer the following questions in your books.

1 What typographical device does Terry Pratchett use in the novel version to suggest the power and presence of Death?

2 How does the artist (Graham Higgins) adapt this device in his drawings?

3 Why do you think Death has a sword in the graphic version and a scytheblade in the novel?

4 Mort's eyes are highlighted in the graphic version by being given a frame to themselves. Write down the sentence from the novel that you think caused Graham Higgins to draw attention to them in this way.

5 Why do you think we are shown the relative heights of Death and Mort in the moment before Mort is supposed to die?

6 Compare the written description of the final grain of sand falling with the illustration. Which do you find the more dramatic?

7 In the novel it says 'the sound of [Death's] laughter rattled the universe'. How well is this idea conveyed by the picture of Death laughing?

8 Draw your own image of Death turning over the hourglass. How would you show that this is a very important moment in the story?

C **SPEAKING AND LISTENING**   READING   WRITING

In pairs, discuss which version of this story you prefer. Think of reasons for your opinions and be prepared to share them with the rest of the class. Consider the following.

● How well do the two stories convey the strength, power and inevitability of death?

● The most striking thing in the story is the fact that Death relents and gives Mort a second chance. Why does he do this? How well is this communicated in the two versions of the story?

Review

Both Terry Pratchett and Graham Higgins want to show an ordinary human being facing up to death. As a class, discuss which version shows Mort's bravery most clearly.

Homework
Write your own version of this scene as a film storyboard.

Biased or objective?

Aims

- To recognise **bias** and **objectivity** in news reports.
- To distinguish facts from opinions.

Starter session

Discuss the following statements with a partner and then write down whether each one is a fact or an opinion.

- Everest is the highest mountain on earth.
- Everest is the earth's most challenging mountain climb.
- Liverpool FC are the most successful team in English football history.
- The novel is most successful in its treatment of the heroine.
- All my friends wish they were taller.
- All my friends are taller than me.

Introduction

Many people assume that the 'news' is the same as the 'facts'. However, even when the information is based on fact, the way it is presented can reveal bias. In this unit we will be looking at how the arrangement, layout and language of news stories can affect our response to them.

KEY TERMS

Bias is the tendency to take one side rather than another in a debate or argument, because of your personal opinion.

Objectivity is the ability to be fair and undistorted by emotion or personal bias.

Development

A **SPEAKING AND LISTENING** **READING** **WRITING**

Read the following text from the BBC News website and answer the questions that follow.

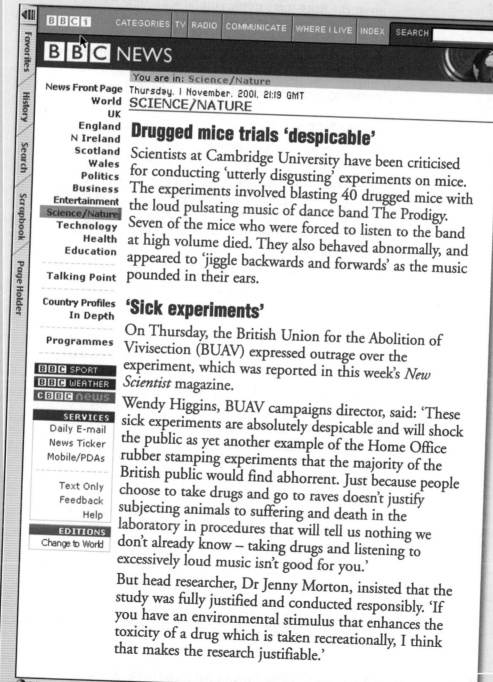

BBC NEWS

You are in: Science/Nature

Thursday, 1 November, 2001, 21:19 GMT

SCIENCE/NATURE

Drugged mice trials 'despicable'

Scientists at Cambridge University have been criticised for conducting 'utterly disgusting' experiments on mice. The experiments involved blasting 40 drugged mice with the loud pulsating music of dance band The Prodigy. Seven of the mice who were forced to listen to the band at high volume died. They also behaved abnormally, and appeared to 'jiggle backwards and forwards' as the music pounded in their ears.

'Sick experiments'

On Thursday, the British Union for the Abolition of Vivisection (BUAV) expressed outrage over the experiment, which was reported in this week's *New Scientist* magazine.

Wendy Higgins, BUAV campaigns director, said: 'These sick experiments are absolutely despicable and will shock the public as yet another example of the Home Office rubber stamping experiments that the majority of the British public would find abhorrent. Just because people choose to take drugs and go to raves doesn't justify subjecting animals to suffering and death in the laboratory in procedures that will tell us nothing we don't already know – taking drugs and listening to excessively loud music isn't good for you.'

But head researcher, Dr Jenny Morton, insisted that the study was fully justified and conducted responsibly. 'If you have an environmental stimulus that enhances the toxicity of a drug which is taken recreationally, I think that makes the research justifiable.'

News Front Page
World
UK
England
N Ireland
Scotland
Wales
Politics
Business
Entertainment
Science/Nature
Technology
Health
Education

Talking Point

Country Profiles
In Depth

Programmes

BBC SPORT
BBC WEATHER
CBBC news

SERVICES
Daily E-mail
News Ticker
Mobile/PDAs

Text Only
Feedback
Help

EDITIONS
Change to World

Internet zone

rites | History | Search | Scrapbook | Page Holder

Inject animals

She said it was part of a wider investigation into the long-term toxic effects of amphetamines, which are still largely unknown.

A total of 238 mice were used in the experiment, conducted at Cambridge four years ago – the results were published in August in the journal *NeuroReport*. Mice given the drug methamphetamine – a strong form of 'speed' taken in clubs – were exposed to silence, white noise, or loud music either by The Prodigy or Bach's Violin Concerto in A minor, which has a similar tempo. Animals injected with salt water instead of methamphetamine fell asleep when exposed to the music.

'Pulsating noise'

But the sound dramatically affected the drugged mice, causing them to suffer more brain damage from the speed than normal. Scientists concluded that loud pulsating music seemed to strengthen the toxic effects of methamphetamine in mice. As well as the seven Prodigy fatalities, four of the 40 mice made to listen to Bach also died.

Dr Morton said on Thursday that the volume used – 95 decibels – was equivalent to listening to a personal stereo turned up reasonably loud. She added the nature of the music was irrelevant, and said it was the 'pulsating noise' that was important. She said the only other attempt to investigate the effect of noise on amphetamine toxicity was a crude experiment conducted in 1942 which involved the researcher banging a filing cabinet near a group of mice. Dr Morton said: 'Amphetamines are taken recreationally in clubs and by people like truck drivers who expose themselves to loud noise. These experiments were done as part of a larger study into the effect of amphetamine on the striatum, a part of the brain which degenerates in Huntingdon's disease. If you have an environmental stimulus that enhances the toxicity of a drug which is taken recreationally, I think that makes the research justifiable.'

She added: 'This experiment was done only once, and we would not have used other animals unnecessarily.'

From http://news.bbc.co.uk/2/hi/uk_news/england/1633252.stm

1 What attitude to the experiments is shown by the use of the word 'despicable' in the headline?

2 Why do you think the BBC has put the word in inverted commas?

3 What other negative quotation is used in the first paragraph of the article? What do you think is the effect on the reader's attitude of these quotations appearing early on?

4 What attitude to the scientist's work is shown by the article's use of the phrases 'forced to listen to' and 'pounded in their ears'?

5 Whose comments are reported first in the article – the experimenters or those of people opposed to the experiments? How is this likely to affect the reader's response?

6 What overall impression do the three subheadings used in the article give?

7 When are the details of the experiment given?

8 When is the strongest health-related justification for the research given? Do newspapers normally expect readers to read this far?

9 With a partner, discuss whether you think this article is an unbiased piece of reporting. What attempts have been made to make the article more balanced? Are they effective?

B SPEAKING AND LISTENING   **READING**   **WRITING**

Read the following two articles, which are taken from publications aimed at young people, and answer the questions.

Scientists organise mouse mash-up*

Researchers at Cambridge University give mice speed, play loud music and watch what happens.

KEY WORD

Mash-up – state of drug-induced euphoria. Also means 'in a very bad condition, messed up'.

Nov 05, 2001

In an effort to find out how music affects the way methamphetamines are absorbed by the body, Cambridge researchers have been dosing mice up with speed and playing very loud music at them. One group of mice were played Bach at a loud volume while the other was played selected Prodigy tracks. They discovered that the effects of the drugs were much more severe when the dance music was played, with only four mouse fatalities (out of a group of forty mice) during the Bach experiment, but seven deaths during the Prodigy session.

However, it was noted that both sets of drugged-up mice displayed the 'disturbing behaviour' of staying in one spot and swaying back and forth while the music played. Researcher Jenny Morton said 'It seems that listening to pulsating music strengthens the toxic effects of methamphetamine ... if you saw how the mice were behaving, you wouldn't want to take any.'

Reports that the mice felt an increased sense of empathy with one another are as yet unconfirmed.

Mickey never knew the pear was laced with speed.

Internet zone

From Spaced – clubbers' website (www.spaced.co.uk)

1 What attitude to the research is shown by the headline and its subheading?

2 What attitude to drug-taking is shown by the mouse photograph and its caption?

3 Compare the way the research is reported here with the BBC story – is there any concern shown for the suffering of the mice?

4 How much prominence is given to the health-related message of the research?

NOISE ANNOYS!

Mice fed speed and exposed to The Prodigy at high volumes died in an experiment to discover whether amphetamines were dangerous in a club environment. The tests, at Cambridge University, also involved mice on drugs having to endure a deafening Bach Violin Concerto in A minor – which the scientists said had a similar tempo to The Prodigy – white noise and silence.

Mouse manipulator Jenny Morton, at the university's Department Of Pharmacology, found that loud music in itself did not harm the rodents as those injected with salt water rather than Class As fell asleep during the experiment. But when injected with speed, seven out of 40 of the mice listening to the Prodigy died. Four out of 40 then keeled over after being exposed to Bach. Morton, however, said the mice could not tell the difference between classical and The Prodigy, who she quaintly described as 'rave'.

She told *New Scientist*: 'They just heard pulsating noise.' She continued that mice on speed usually ran round for half an hour, before descending into a rapid, repetitive movement called stereotypy, then charged around for another half an hour before becoming normal again. She also found the mice suffered more brain damage from the combination of speed and 'pulsating music' than by speed or music alone. She concluded: 'If you saw how the mice behaved, you wouldn't want to take methamphetamine (speed). I might go to raves, but I wouldn't take methamphetamine.'

From *New Musical Express* 14th November 2001

5 The mice who died are said to have 'keeled over'. What attitude to the death of the mice does this indicate?

6 Why is the researcher's use of the word 'raves' described as quaint? Why do you think this is?

7 What conclusions about health and drug use are readers meant to come to after reading this report? Why is this conclusion given in the words of the researcher, rather than as part of the article?

Review

As a class, discuss whether it is possible to report the news in a completely unbiased way. How should we as readers guard against biased opinions?

Homework

Write an article reporting this experiment for a health magazine. Your article should reflect the views that might be supported by such a magazine.

Cartoons, films and comics

Aims

- To investigate how meanings are changed when information is presented in different forms or transferred into different media.

Starter session

With a partner, discuss the meaning of the word 'free' in the phrase 'free gifts' and the sentence 'Free the whale.'

- Where would you expect to see 'free gifts'?
- Where might you see 'Free the whale'?
- How much does the context affect your understanding of the words? For instance, what would you assume if you saw a sign saying 'Free Holiday' next to a picture of a man behind bars?
- Report your ideas back to the class.

Introduction

We understand texts in different ways and we apply different rules according to the type of text we are 'reading'. For example, we accept that the cartoon character Wiley Coyote can fall into a canyon and survive, but we also accept that the heroines of *Thelma and Louise* are about to fall to their deaths when they drive their car into the Grand Canyon at the end of the film.

In this unit we will be looking at how the conventions of different media affect our responses to similar ideas. We will also consider what happens when we adapt stories from one medium into another.

Development

In recent years there have been a number of adaptations of cartoons into live-action feature films. Films such as *Batman*, *Superman*, *The X-Men* and *Spiderman* began life as comic books, but there have also been live-action versions of *The Flintstones*, *Scooby Doo* and *Inspector Gadget*.

A **SPEAKING AND LISTENING** READING WRITING

1 With a partner, discuss why you think Hollywood film studios have been prepared to invest hundreds of millions of dollars in such projects.
2 What audiences do such films appeal to?

B SPEAKING AND LISTENING **READING** **WRITING**

Inspector Gadget began life as an animated cartoon and was produced as a live-action film, starring Matthew Broderick, in 2000.

With a partner, study the storyboard on page 74 from a scene in the film, then answer the questions below.

1 What does the first point of view (pov) shot establish for the audience?
2 What elements of the scene reflect the animated cartoon origin of the story?
3 What is the main difference for an audience between watching the action shown as an animated cartoon and with live actors?
4 Almost half of the panels show close-ups of the actors' faces. Why do you think this is?
5 Would there have been so many close-ups in a cartoon version?
6 Why is there a close-up of the umbrella opening?
7 How do the suggested camera movements help to create a sense of speed and danger?
8 The storyboard begins with a moment of fear for the two characters. Describe how the mood of the scene changes as the storyboard progresses.

SPEAKING AND LISTENING

A further important difference between a live-action film and an animated film is the cost of production.

1 Is there any difference between the cost of animating this scene and animating a scene in which Inspector Gadget walks into a room?

2 How many people do you think would be required to film the live-action version of this scene? Think about the camera crews and other technicians, the actors and stunt doubles, the director, and the people involved in post-production and special effects.

3 How do you think cost implications affect what live-action directors can produce?

Review

As a class, discuss whether you think people who enjoyed *Inspector Gadget* as an animated cartoon are certain to enjoy *Inspector Gadget* as a film. If not, why not? What extra things are there to think about when watching a live-action film? How many of the live-action film adaptations of cartoons that you have seen would you say have been successful?

Homework

Imagine you are a Hollywood film producer with a budget of $50 million to spend on one of the following:

● an film with an original script
● an adaptation of a successful comic book
● an adaptation of a successful animated cartoon
● an adaptation of a best-selling novel.

Explain which project you would choose and why you think it would be successful. Think about the similarities and differences between the comic/cartoon/novel and your film version. Which features would be carried across and which would be lost or changed?

Texts and technology

Aims

● To look at how texts are shaped by the technology they use.

Starter session

Most activities have their own special language or jargon. Write out the following list of words related to computer gaming and try to explain each one:

● shoot-'em-up
● platform game
● Play Station

● RPG
● role-play game
● God game

● 40 gigabyte hard drive
● 1st person shoot-'em-up
● real-time strategy game.

Introduction

Computer games have come a long way since they first appeared in the 1970s. There are now dozens of different types of games and thousands of different titles to choose from. Even simple graphics cards have more processing power and memory than was used in the spacecraft that went to the moon. In this unit we will be looking at computer games and identifying some of the features that make them unique.

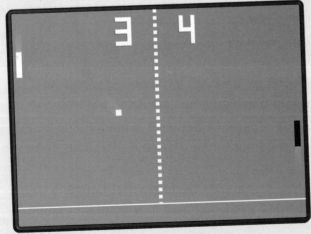

An exciting 1970s computer game.

Development

Read the following extract from an article by 13-year-old Joshua Stamp-Simon, which was published in *The Guardian*.

Games

Trigger Happy

[...] My favourite type of computer game [is] the RPG. This stands for role-playing game, not rocket-propelled grenade or rancid poultry guts. As you may have guessed, in a role-playing game you take on the role of a character. Or several characters. RPGs are generally centred around violence. But even where enjoyment is solely derived from fighting, such as Diablo II, there is a distinct difference between RPGs and the standard shoot-'em-up. The difference is that you make choices about the character you are playing, in terms of appearance, race, class, skills and so on.

Being able to make these choices is the main reason that I like RPGs. If you are reading a book, you may understand a character. In RPGs, you are the character. Just for a few hours, you can be someone else. You can be evil and kill everything in sight, or not, if you wish. When you read a book, the author decides what happens next. You, the reader, are merely finding out. With computer games, you decide what happens.

Of course, the same is true with real life. You make the choices. But it is far easier to do it with someone else's life, especially if that someone is binary on a computer's hard disk. Choices in real life are either boringly simple, such as what to have for breakfast, or mind-bogglingly large, such as what career to pursue. You don't want to mess those up. That's what limits your choices in real life.

This doesn't apply to computer games — and that's why I like them.

1 What is the main appeal of role-playing games for Joshua Stamp-Simon?

2 In your own words, explain the difference between a reader's response to a character in a book and a gamer's response to a character in a role-playing game.

3 Joshua Stamp-Simon says that the author decides what happens in a book, but that the player decides what happens in a computer game. How true is this statement?

4 What does Joshua Stamp-Simon like about making decisions in a computer game as compared to making decisions in real life?

Another view of computer gaming is provided by Jørgen Kirksæther, a doctoral student at the Department of Art and Media Studies at the Norwegian University of Science and Technology in Trondheim.

If you come home with a new game and finish it in a couple of hours, you feel cheated. Since a computer game, at least here in Norway, costs about ten times as much as a movie ticket, you expect it to last a little longer. It doesn't matter if you had a fabulous time those two hours, it just isn't value for money. So, the game designer puts obstacles into the game. They force you to replay game segments until you master them, which in turn moves the game 'story' forward. In a shoot-'em-up this would be like progressing to a new level, in an adventure, like gaining access to new areas. This underlying structure results in something interesting: games are almost never played in straight line, plot-wise. Instead, you move through them in circles. [...] It can be likened to reading a novel where your task is to get to the last chapter, but where skipping sections is not allowed.

When all the logic structures are revealed, one would think that the game would be discarded. For some games, though, this is not true. A completed adventure is seldom booted up again, but another round of PacMan, even after you have figured out Inky and Blinky's every move, is still a blast. Obviously there must be different rewards in playing different types of games. In PacMan's case, one could say that there are two set goals; the low-level one of clearing the board of dots, and the high-level one of clearing as many as possible. How many times can you do this before you've had enough?

Myst, one of the best-selling computer games ever, is a puzzle-based adventure game.

1 How do computer game designers extend the user's gaming experience?

2 How do 'obstacles' affect the 'plot' of a computer game?

3 Why do you think gamers seldom return to completed adventure games? Could the same be said of books you have read once already?

4 What are the rewards of playing PacMan or simple shoot-'em-up games? What are the rewards of reading a book or watching a film?

Final Fantasy is an extremely successful series of computer games – Final Fantasy XII is currently available. In 2001 a film based on the games was released. *Final Fantasy: The Spirit Within* featured ground-breaking computer-generated characters, but it was not well received. Here is part of a review of the film from the BBCi website.

1 What does the reviewer see as the major fault of the film?

2 What other faults are mentioned?

3 Do you think these faults would have caused a problem if the film had been an interactive computer game?

4 What are the most important elements of a computer game? What about the most important elements of a good film? Can you think of any reasons why making a computer game into a film might be unsuccessful?

> The story is a functional slice of science fiction, as scientist Aki Ross (Ming-Na) and mentor Dr Sid (Sutherland) work with a 'Deep Eyes' marine unit (Baldwin, Buscemi, Rhames) to defeat wraith-like aliens by channelling the eight 'spirit waves' of Earth or Gaia, the planetary soul. Yet like so much of Japan's Anime output, it's long on imagination and short on story.
>
> With a plot that freely plunders the likes of *Aliens* and *Starship Troopers*, the visual grandeur cannot hide clichéd dialogue, thin characters, and a frustrating lack of development. Where most blockbusters would go for the big-bang ending, *Final Fantasy* is content to indulge its spiritualist angle, resulting in a damp 'healing power of love' conclusion, replete with pointless sacrifice.

5 Why do you think the makers of the film *Final Fantasy: The Spirit Within* felt the need to avoid a dramatic ending?

Review

With a partner, make two lists – one of the major differences between computer games and books, and the other of the major differences between computer games and films. Discuss the advantages and disadvantages of the three media types using examples from books, films and computer games that you are familiar with. Be prepared to discuss your ideas with the rest of the class.

Homework

Briefly outline the plot of a simple adventure story. Explain what you would need to add to the plot if you were making the story into a computer game.

Who can you trust?

Aims

- To look at how texts are structured.
- To look at how content is organised.
- To look at what patterns of language are used.

Starter session

Match the following structures to the texts that use them most often.

alphabetical order	Hollywood film
beginning, middle, end	play
headline, main points, details	story
introduction, low point, high point, low point, high point	sonnet
act 1, scene 1; act 2, etc.	newspaper article
storyline 1, storyline 2, storyline 3, storyline 4, etc.	dictionary
octave, volta, sestet	soap opera

Compare your answers with a partner's. Are any of these structures applicable in more than one genre or text type?

Introduction

In any text, you have to be able to find your way around. This is easiest in a dictionary or an encyclopaedia, where alphabetical order is used, but even in the most complex text there has to be some underlying organising principle. Perhaps the most chaotic texts we meet on a regular basis are magazines. The word 'magazine' comes from an Arabic term for a storehouse – most magazines are complex collections of pictures, fiction and articles. In this unit we will be looking at how magazines are organised.

Before we start, make a list with a partner of the sections that you can find in most magazines.

Development

 A SPEAKING AND LISTENING **READING** **WRITING**

The first thing people see when they pick up a magazine is its front cover. Look at the cover of the magazine below and then answer the questions.

1 How much of the cover is given over to features that are unique to this edition?

2 Does the cover tell you anything about parts that occur in every edition?

3 Which part of the cover of this magazine might make you want to read it?

Once you have picked up a magazine because something mentioned on the cover has caught your eye, your next port of call might be the contents page. Below are two contents pages from very different magazines: *Real* and *Total DVD*.

4 How are the pages organised?

5 What do the contents pages of the two magazines have in common?

6 What is the biggest difference between the two magazines?

7 How are the magazines arranged so that regular readers can find their favourite sections?

■ The stories on this issue's cover

TRENDS

FEATURES

STYLE DIRECTORY

VITAL SELF

FOOD & INTERIORS

REGULARS

FEATURES

SOFTWARE

HARDWARE

REGULARS

1 With a partner, discuss how you actually use magazines. Do you:

- flick through the magazine looking for parts that catch your eye?
- look first for the article from the cover that attracted your attention?
- check the contents page and find articles that interest you there?
- turn straight to the sections that you know you enjoy?

Be prepared to discuss your strategies with the rest of the class.

Within a magazine we can identify a number of distinctive article types. These include:

- letters from readers
- reviews and consumer advice
- 'How to' articles
- interviews
- problem pages
- longer 'feature' articles on a particular topic
- news items
- editorial comments
- columns by a particular journalist, an expert or a celebrity
- horoscopes, puzzles and other 'fun' features.

In addition, of course, almost all magazines contain a great deal of advertising.

2 How many of these article types can you identify in the contents pages shown?

Review

You should now know a great deal about the way magazines are put together. In small groups, discuss how language used on the covers and in contents pages makes you want to read more. For instance, how many of the listings ask questions? How many use imperative verbs like 'discover'? How many simply provide you with the information? Be prepared to share your ideas with the whole class.

Homework

Design the cover and contents page of a magazine that would interest you. Try to make it as realistic as possible.

Year 8 SATs

The Real Moby Dick

On November 20th, 1820, the whale-ship Essex was attacked and sunk by a sperm whale. The crew were stranded thousands of miles away from land and endured great hardships before eight of them were rescued. Their story inspired Herman Melville's novel Moby Dick. The following extract is from the account written by the first mate of the Essex, Owen Chase.

… I observed a very large spermaceti whale, as well as I could judge about eighty five feet in length. He broke water about twenty rods off our weather bow and was lying quietly, with his head in a direction for the ship. He spouted two or three times and then disappeared. In less than two or three seconds, he came up again, about the length of the ship off, and made directly for us at the rate of about three knots. The ship was then going with about the same velocity. His appearance and attitude gave us at first no alarm, but while I stood watching his movements and observing him, but a ship's length off, coming down for us with great celerity, I involuntarily ordered the boy at the helm to put it hard up, intending to sheer off and avoid him.

The words were scarcely out of my mouth before he came down upon us with full speed and struck the ship with his head, just forward of the fore chains. He gave us such an appalling and tremendous jar as nearly threw us all on our faces. The ship brought up as suddenly and violently as if she had struck a rock and trembled for a few seconds like a leaf.

We looked at each other with perfect amazement, deprived almost of the power of speech. Many minutes elapsed before we were able to realize the dreadful accident. During this time the whale passed under the ship, grazing her keel as he went along. He came up alongside of her to leeward and lay on the top of the water, apparently stunned with the violence of the blow, for the space of a minute. He then suddenly started off in a direction to leeward.

After a few moments' reflection and recovering, in some measure, from the sudden consternation that had seized us, I of course concluded that he had stove a hole in the ship and that it would be necessary to set the pumps going. Accordingly, they were rigged but had not been in operation more than one minute before I perceived the head of the ship to be gradually settling down in the water. I then … discovered the whale, apparently in convulsions, on the top of the water about one hundred rods to leeward. He was enveloped in the foam of the sea that his continual and violent thrashing about in the water had created around him, and I could distinctly see him smite his jaws together, as if distracted with rage and fury. He remained a short time in this situation and then started off with great velocity across the bow of the ship to windward.

By this time the ship had settled down a considerable distance in the water, and I gave her up as lost. I, however, ordered the pumps to be kept constantly going and endeavoured to collect my thoughts for the occasion. ...While my attention was thus engaged for a moment, I was aroused with the cry of a man at the hatchway: "Here he is – he is making for us again."

I turned around and saw him, about one hundred rods directly ahead of us, coming down apparently with twice his ordinary speed and, it appeared to me at that moment, with tenfold fury and vengeance in his aspect. The surf flew in all directions about him, and his course towards us was marked by white foam a rod in width, which he made with the continual violent thrashing of his tail. His head was about half out of water, and in that way he came upon and again struck the ship.

I should judge the speed of the ship to have been at this time about three knots and that of the whale about six. He struck her to windward, and completely stove in her bow. He passed under the ship again, went off to leeward, and we saw no more of him.

Our situation at this juncture can be more readily imagined than described. The shock to our feelings was such as I am sure none can have an adequate conception of that were not there. The misfortune befell us at a moment when we least dreamt of any accident. From the pleasing anticipations we had formed of realizing the certain profits of our labour, we were dejected by a sudden, most mysterious, and overwhelming calamity.

From *The Wreck of the Whaleship Essex* – Owen Chase

Whale sanctuaries overview

Last edited: 2001-11-20

Whales face threats from many sources, including pollution and climate change, but they are most directly threatened by commercial whale hunting. (1100 were killed for profit in 1998 alone, and the numbers are increasing every year – we'll work out how many were killed in 2000 and point out this number looks set to increase.)

Sanctuaries – a safe place, a place of refuge – give whales freedom from one of these threats: commercial whaling. Greenpeace wants to strengthen current protection for whales by implementing a series of regional sanctuaries, which will act as stepping stones in the longer term towards a Global Whale Sanctuary and a permanent end to all commercial whaling.

Press F...

- Global
  urges
  hunt i...
- South
  Sanctuary blocked again
- Eastern Caribbean
  supports whale sanctuary

Related Stories

- Oceans campaign homepage
- Victory! Mexican whale sanctuary declared
- Victory! Mexican whale sanctuary declared

Moving Images

- Whale sanctuaries

Building on the present

The body responsible for ensuring the healthy state of whale populations, the International Whaling Commission, agreed in 1979 to establish the Indian Ocean Whale Sanctuary, protecting whales in their breeding and calving grounds. Fifteen years later, in 1994, the IWC established the Southern Ocean Sanctuary. This covers all waters surrounding Antarctica and protects three-quarters of the world's whales in their feeding grounds.

At the 1998 meeting of the IWC, plans for two further sanctuaries were put forward. These included the South Pacific Whale Sanctuary, suggested by Australia and New Zealand and the South Atlantic Sanctuary, proposed by Brazil. If accepted, these new sanctuaries would start where the Southern Ocean Sanctuary ends.

Extending protection for the great whales

This coverage from the freezing waters of the Antarctic to the warm waters of the equator is vital. Most of the great whales are highly migratory, feeding in the nutrient-rich waters of the Antarctic before travelling to tropical waters to give birth and suckle their young. They then make the long migration back to their feeding grounds.

Since whales rarely cross the equator, establishment of these sanctuaries would mean that the whales of the Southern Hemisphere could live their entire lives in an area free from commercial whaling.

Whale watching: commerce without killing

In addition to promoting research and conservation, sanctuaries will help encourage whale watching and the industry that develops around it. Increasing numbers of people who have seen whales in their natural habitat are supporting global shelter for them. They want to see the whales they watch protected, not being hunted.

Message of hope

Sanctuaries are a forward-thinking measure. They make economic sense, help protect whales and encourage research on whales and the environment. They send a clear message of hope that the world is turning away from whaling and that there will be no return to the commercial hunting which devastated one population after another.

http://www.greenpeace.org.uk/contentlookup.cfm?CFID=442594&CFTOKEN=42952582&SitekeyParam=D-H-B

Year 8 Test Questions

Answer the following questions in your books.

Questions 1–4 are about *The Real Moby Dick*.

1 From the first paragraph, write down the speed at which the ship and the whale struck each other.

(1 mark)

2 In the second paragraph, how does the author convey the force of the blow?

(1 mark)

3 In paragraphs three the author describes the response of both the crew and the whale to the attack.

   a Pick out two phrases which show these responses.

(2 marks)

   b In what way are the responses similar?

(1 mark)

4 In the whole text, how does the writer give a sense of the unexpectedness of the whale's attack?
You should comment on how the writer:
- sets the scene
- shows the reactions of the crew
- comments on what has taken place. *(5 marks)*

Questions 5–8 are about the fact sheet *Whale Sanctuaries Overview*.

5 From paragraph 1, give two of the ways in which the survival of whales is being threatened. *(2 marks)*

6 Sum up the reasons why it is important that whale sanctuaries cover both warm and cold oceans. *(2 marks)*

7 In the whole fact sheet, explain how the writer uses facts and figures to persuade readers that whale sanctuaries are a good idea. *(5 marks)*

8 How effective is the picture used in the fact sheet in supporting its argument for whale watching sanctuaries?
How does the writer use headings to make the text clearer and easy to follow? *(2 marks)*

Question 9 is about *The Real Moby Dick* and *Whale Sanctuaries Overview*.

9 The Real Moby Dick and Whale Sanctuaries Overview are very different texts.
Copy out and complete the table below, suggesting:
- one purpose of each text
- one word or phrase to describe the language used in each text.

	The Real Moby Dick	*Whale Sanctuaries Overview*
Purpose of text		
Language used in the text		

(2 marks)

Smoke without fire?

Aims

● To evaluate the relevance, reliability and validity of information available through different media sources.

Starter session

Do this quick quiz. Where would you go for the following items of information? As your teacher reads out each item, write down the best place to find:

● football scores while the matches are still being played
● a summary of football scores when all the matches are over
● a full account of a football game
● the latest gossip on your favourite TV, film or pop stars
● a preview of a soon-to-be-released album track.

Compare your answers with other members of the class.

Introduction

Information can come from hundreds of different sources and can be in all sorts of formats. When looking for information, you need to ask yourself key questions about how to judge the quality of the information and how close it is to what you actually need. In this unit we will be applying our knowledge of the media to help to answer these questions when trying to find out information on the subject of smoking.

Development

SPEAKING AND LISTENING **READING** **WRITING**

A key question that we should apply to all media is 'Who produced it and why?' Information is not free, and so it is sensible to ask why someone has gone to the trouble of providing it. A simple example of this can be seen if you look at the following heading from the opening pages of two websites on smoking.

Action on Smoking and Health
A National Charitable Anti-smoking & Non-smokers' Rights Organisation

1 What information does ASH provide about where their money comes from?

2 What information does FOREST provide at this point about its funding?

3 In 2001 96% of FOREST's £300,000 a year budget came from the cigarette industry. Why do you think FOREST fails to mention this at the start of its website?

4 How might knowledge of its funding affect your response to the information provided by FOREST?

5 How might the statement that ASH is a charity affect your response to the information it provides?

B **SPEAKING AND LISTENING** **READING** **WRITING**

The next question we should ask is 'What type of text is it?' This might seem obvious, but advertising in particular often uses a variety of text types to get its message across. The following page appeared in a number of American magazines.

Movie stars don't have to find a cure for cancer.
But at least they could stop causing it.

Big Tobacco is the leading preventable cause of death. Yet stars like Julia Roberts and Brad Pitt glamorize its deadly products by smoking on screen in films shown worldwide. Think how much good they could do if they simply quit smoking in their movies. Given the evidence, wouldn't you?

Julia Roberts and Brad Pitt have influenced young audiences to smoke in at least four movies each. Will their most lasting legacy be hundreds of thousands of deaths? Or a principled refusal to do Big Tobacco's dirty work?

Over the next twelve months, the tobacco industry will kill more women and men in the U.S. than AIDS, drunk driving, illegal drugs, homicide and suicide *combined*.

Over the next ten years, more than fifty million people will die of tobacco-related diseases worldwide: heart disease, emphysema, cancer.

One in seven kids worldwide gets hooked by age fifteen. Most want to quit now; most will fail. One in three will end up dead from their addiction.

Every day in the United States, two thousand more teens become addicted to tobacco. Smoking is growing even faster in the developing world, where awareness of the dangers is lowest and Big Tobacco's marketing tactics are uncontrolled.

Both in the U.S. and overseas, American movies are a key vehicle for promoting tobacco addiction.

On screens as big as billboards and on millions of videos, U.S. movies in the 1990s showed more smoking than in half a century — with more stars promoting specific brands.

80% of top-grossing PG13 movies and video releases from 1996 to 2000 featured smoking. Tobacco's screen time in those youth-targeted movies climbed 50% over the same period.

Just how influential are stars who smoke? Recent studies show that if a teenager's favorite movie star smokes on screen, he or she is significantly more likely to actually start smoking — even if friends and family don't.

Big Tobacco knows the power of movies. Ten years ago, it was paying to place its products on screen while denying it to Congress. It denies paying today, too. But do tobacco companies even pretend to protest when trademarked brands appear in the hands of stars like Julia Roberts or Brad Pitt? Don't hold your breath.

Either stars are trading favors with Big Tobacco, in which case they're corrupt. Or they're pumping up Big Tobacco's profits for free, in which case they're stupid.

As more young fans realize that nothing winds up on screen by accident, they're asking stars to stop doing Big Tobacco's dirty work. The stars owe it to their audience to listen.

Here are other powerful ways for Hollywood to get unhooked from Big Tobacco:

1] ROLL ON-SCREEN CREDITS IN SMOKING FILMS certifying that nobody on a production accepted *anything* of value from any tobacco company, its agents or fronts.

2] RUN STRONG ANTI-TOBACCO ADS IN FRONT OF SMOKING MOVIES. On tapes and DVDs, too. Strong spots are proven to immunize audiences.

3] QUIT IDENTIFYING TOBACCO BRANDS in the background *or* in action. Brand names are unnecessary.

4] RATE NEW SMOKING MOVIES "R" to give parents more power to protect children against the tobacco industry.

Get the inside story at SmokeFreeMovies.ucsf.edu

Smoke Free Movies aims to sharply reduce the film industry's usefulness to Big Tobacco's domestic and global marketing — a leading cause of disability and premature death. This initiative by Stanton Glantz, PhD (coauthor of *The Cigarette Papers* and *Tobacco War*) of the UCSF School of Medicine is supported by the Robert Wood Johnson Foundation and the Richard and Rhoda Goldman Fund. To learn how you can help, visit our website or write to us: Smoke Free Movies, UCSF School of Medicine, Box 1390, San Francisco, CA 94145-1390.

1 What text type does this seem to be?

2 What type of text is it?

3 Why do you think the information about the purpose of the page is provided at the bottom?

4 Does the fact that this 'article' is sponsored by an anti-smoking group make the information it provides any less valid?

5 How does knowing that you are reading an advertisement rather than an article affect your response to the information?

How a text is produced can often communicate something about the importance of its message.

1 How does the fact that an image appears on a billboard affect its impact?
2 How easy is it to ignore a billboard compared with, say, an advert in a magazine?
3 What message about a product is communicated by the fact that its manufacturers can afford to mount a poster campaign?

D **SPEAKING AND LISTENING   READING**   WRITING

Texts about smoking can be very complex, and so the question 'How does a text create meaning?' is not a simple one. The following text is from a journal for health professionals called *Health Matters*.

Why a few tips won't go far

Recent anti-smoking campaigns ignore the psychological nature of smoking, say Catherine Sykes and David Marks.

What do you get if you mix an old Health Education Authority leaflet with a bit of gloss, some colour and widespread publicity? Answer: the recent NHS 'Don't give up giving up' smoking cessation campaign.

This campaign is based on the *Stopping Smoking Made Easier* leaflet published in 1992, a simplified application of the well-known health psychology model of health behaviour change. But remove the gloss and all that remains are several snippets of advice on smoking cessation. Are we wrong to have doubts about some of the advice offered? Can you really imagine that dry cleaning your clothes, getting your teeth polished and asking family and friends to sponsor your quit attempt will be helpful to smokers, especially those from lower socio-economic backgrounds? It certainly does not fit with our experience of the many smokers with whom we have worked. Doing something else or avoiding situations where you smoke is inappropriate advice. What are you supposed to do if – like many smokers – you smoke after a meal? Avoid eating?

Working in pairs, discuss the following.

1 What kind of text is this? How can you tell?

2 What is the audience for this text? How can you tell?

3 What criticism does the text offer of the 'Don't give up giving up' campaign?

4 Does the criticism concern the presentation of the information, the information itself, or both?

5 Why do you think the authors use so many questions in the second paragraph?

6 Look at the phrases 'Are we wrong to have doubts ...?' and 'Can you really imagine ...?'. What is the purpose of such phrases as these?

Review

A knowledge of the media and how it works can help you to find, understand and interpret information correctly. As a class, discuss what you think are the most important issues that you have to bear in mind when researching a controversial topic.

Homework

Write a set of guidelines for people who are about to research a controversial topic. Give at least five pieces of advice, supported by examples if possible.

Newspapers and their audiences

Aims

- To look at how media texts influence and are influenced by their readers.

Starter session

Have you ever done any of the following:

- voted in a newspaper poll?
- nominated a Big Brother contestant for eviction?
- made a contribution to the 'notice board' section of a website?
- written an online review of a book at a site like amazon.co.uk?
- used the interactive button on your digital handset?
- written a letter to a newspaper?

If you have done any of these things, you have had some idea of how 'interactive' media texts work.

With a partner, look at the following reasons why media texts are sometimes interactive and match them to the list above:

- to earn money (e.g. from premium-rate phone calls)
- to make users of the text feel that their contributions are welcome
- to involve people more closely in an event or campaign
- to gain information about what users think
- to make the sharing of ideas and information a two-way process. `

Introduction

We can tell something about the audience of a text by looking at what the producers think will interest their audience. For instance, when Lady Diana Spencer married Prince Charles in 1982 the wedding was front-page news in almost all British newspapers, but the *Morning Star*, a communist newspaper, carried only a small paragraph about traffic delays.

With a partner, discuss why you think the *Morning Star* chose to focus on traffic disruption rather than the wedding.

In this unit, we are going to consider how the coverage of various stories in two different newspapers gives us information about their audiences.

Development

Below is a table which compares the stories that appeared in the early parts of *The Daily Express* and *The Guardian* on 29th August 2002. This date has been chosen because no one story dominated the headlines on that day. Major stories at the time included the continuing investigation into the murder of two ten-year-old girls, worries about the possibilities of war with Iraq and various health-, education- and police-related scandals.

A *SPEAKING AND LISTENING*   *READING*   *WRITING*

Look carefully at the two lists and then answer the questions that follow.

Page	The Daily Express	The Guardian
1.	**Maxine to escape mob** A suspect in a murder case to give evidence by video link to avoid public protest.	**Pressure on Bush to back off** President Bush urged not to attack Iraq. **Voters attack Labour's green record** Report on opinion poll. **EU promises more cash for Africa** Earth Summit resolution. **The Codfather and the offer a publisher should have refused** Legal case with 'mafia' connections.
2.	**Nine motors for two Jags** John Prescott, deputy Prime Minister has access to nine cars. **2 cops paid £32,500 to do nothing** Police corruption enquiry. **Minders back new code for the royals** Security arrangements for the royal family.	**£4bn deal to save Marconi** Business news. **Carr to give evidence by video link** A suspect in a murder case – to give evidence by video link to avoid public protest. **Corruption will never be wiped out, Met admits** Police corruption enquiry. **The Codfather and the offer a publisher should have refused** (continued) Legal case with 'mafia' connections.
3.	**How I nearly broke the poor camel's back** Human interest story – woman loses weight after embarrassing camel ride.	**Searching for a hero: why America has turned to Winston Churchill** Background feature on US response to war on terrorism.
4.	**Kidneys for cash** Doctor accused making a profit out of arranging organ donations.	**'Put the thirst of poor communities first,' demands Mandela** Nelson Mandela calls for better arrangements for water supplies.

	Buy-to-let fuels boom House prices are increasing. **Probe boss steps down** **Teachers not cleared** Problems caused by delays in checking the police records of teachers.		US blocks moves to give powers to those threatened by multinationals Earth Summit report. Big business and Greenpeace urge action on climate change Earth Summit report.
5.	Who's that guy kissing Kylie's man? – exclusive A story about Kylie Minogue's boyfriend.		Met chief admits faults in Damilola case Enquiry report on police handling of a murder enquiry. **BBC goes to extreme to fill its Grandstand** BBC to show 'extreme' sports. **Row over 'Nazi' name on trainers** Inappropriate name on trainers. **Online tax returns doomed, MPs warn** Online tax returns not popular because of concerns about Internet security.
6.	So hard for us to say 'forgive' Background story on the murders of two ten-year-old girls. Jail video link to beat hate mob (continued from page 1) A suspect in a murder case to give evidence by video link to avoid public protest.		GP accused of fixing kidney donor for a fee Doctor accused of making a profit out of arranging organ donations. **Children 'hooked within days' of starting smoking** Health report on effects of smoking. **Straw warns left to face reform or face voter apathy** Report on discussions within the Labour party. **Commuters 'are treated worse than cattle' on Tube** Protest at conditions on the London Underground. **Murder hunt for carjackers who ran down soccer fan** Crime story.
7.			Guardian first book award – the longlist Feature on Guardian first book award. **Former gambler makes novel prize longlist** Background on one of the authors on the first book award longlist. **Maths crisis in university admissions** Not enough students are applying for university maths courses. **Pupils told to stay home over police checks** Problems caused by delays in checking the records of teachers.

1 Write a list of the stories that appeared in both newspapers.

2 Which newspaper contains the most human-interest stories?

3 Which newspaper contains the most political stories?

4 Which newspaper has the most foreign news?

5 Which paper would you choose to read for entertainment? Explain your choice.

6 Which paper would you choose for information? Explain your choice.

7 Compare the headline 'Corruption will never be wiped out, Met admits' from *The Guardian* with '2 cops paid £32,500 to do nothing' from *The Daily Express*. Both headlines tell the same story, but what does each headline tell us about reader preferences and attitudes?

8 Page three of a newspaper is the first page that readers see as they open it. It therefore offers a second chance to engage the interest of the readers. How have the editors of the two papers chosen to do this?

9 With a partner, discuss what you can tell about the interests of *Daily Express* readers based on the stories in this edition of the paper.

10 What can you tell about the interests of *Guardian* readers based on this edition of the paper?

B SPEAKING AND LISTENING READING WRITING

The front page of a newspaper is very important, as the lead story on it helps many people to decide which paper to buy on a particular day. Understandably, newspaper editors spend a great deal of time deciding on their front-page lead.

1 With your partner, discuss why you think the editors of *The Express* chose to lead on the story of Maxine Carr. How does this choice reflect the interests of the readers?

2 Why do you think *The Guardian* editors chose the George Bush/Iraq story? What does this decision tell us about *Guardian* readers?

Review

Here are four headlines for major news stories.

1 Queen's corgi kidnapped
2 Tory party in row over Europe
3 American stock market crash
4 British athlete sets new world record

Working in groups, decide which of these stories you would use as the front-page lead for *The Guardian* and which for *The Express*. Be prepared to justify your choices in terms of how you see the audiences for each paper. Choose a story from an evening TV or radio news broadcast and write notes on its main points. Then write *Guardian*- and *Daily Express*-style headlines for it.

Mary Shelley's monster in the media

Aims

- To look at how the same text or idea can be presented in different media.
- To develop critical analysis.

Starter session

Which of the following pictures shows Frankenstein?*

A

B

C

Mary Shelley wrote *Frankenstein, or the Modern Prometheus* in 1818. Within five years the story had been adapted for the stage, and there have been over 50 film and television adaptations since then. With a partner, discuss why you think this story has been adapted so often.

Introduction

Everybody knows the story of *Frankenstein*, or at least a version of it. Dr Frankenstein created a living creature from the parts of dead bodies; however, Mary Shelley did not think of the result of Dr Frankenstein's experiment as a monster. In the original text it is only ever referred to as 'the creature'. In this unit we are going to look at how the creature – and his creator – are represented in a variety of adaptations of the story.

*Answer: C

Development

Here is how Dr Frankenstein reacted to his own experiment in the original text.

I had worked hard for nearly two years, for the sole purpose of infusing life into an inanimate body. For this I had deprived myself of rest and health. I had desired it with an ardour that far exceeded moderation; but now that I had finished, the beauty of the dream vanished, and breathless horror and disgust filled my heart. Unable to endure the aspect of the being I had created, I rushed out of the room and continued a long time traversing my bed-chamber, unable to compose my mind to sleep.

The scientist is unable to stand the sight of the creature he has created and so he allows it to wander off into a nearby forest. Here, the lonely creature observes a poor but honest and cheerful family for over a year, and learns through them to speak and even to read. However, like Frankenstein, the family assumes that the creature's outward appearance reflects an evil nature, and they reject him. The lonely and sensitive creature blames his troubles on Dr Frankenstein.

'Cursed, cursed creator! Why did I live? Why, in that instant, did I not extinguish the spark of existence which you had so wantonly bestowed? I know not; despair had not yet taken possession of me; my feelings were those of rage and revenge.'

When the doctor refuses to make him a female companion the creature murders his creator's family and begins a long chase that ends in the death of both Dr Frankenstein and the creature himself.

1 Does it seem, from the above account, that Mary Shelley intended the creature to be seen as a simple monster?

2 What message about appearance did she intend to convey?

3 What does the fact that Dr Frankenstein is destroyed by the creature tell us about the role of the scientist?

The first film of *Frankenstein* was made in 1910, but probably the most successful version was that made by James Whale in 1931. Boris Karloff played the creature as more of a monster, in make-up that established a look that is still recognised today. The monster is accidentally given an 'abnormal' brain and never learns to speak. It tries to make contact with a blind man and a little girl once it has escaped from Frankenstein's castle, but it is blamed for the little girl's murder (the monster killed her by accident) by a group of peasants who eventually burn it to death. The monster tries to take revenge on its creator shortly before it dies, but Dr Frankenstein survives.

1 Why do you think the film version omitted the creature's desire to have a female companion?

2 In the novel it is clear that the creature becomes bad because of the way he is treated. 'I was benevolent and good; misery made me a fiend. Make me happy, and I shall again be virtuous,' he says. What is the effect of implying that his evil nature is caused by an 'abnormal' brain in the film?

3 Why do you think the film version made the creature into a monster?

4 What comment does the film make on the role of the scientist?

The film *The Curse of Frankenstein*, made in 1957, makes further changes to the story. Dr Frankenstein murders a fellow scientist to obtain his brain, and when his mistress tries to blackmail him, the doctor locks her in the cellar with the creature, who then murders her. As in the 1931 film, the brain received by the monster is damaged.

1 What is the effect of making the doctor into a murderer in this film?

2 What does this change show about attitudes to scientists in the 1950s?

1 What aspect of Mary Shelley's creature does this cover emphasise?

2 What audience do you think would be attracted by this story of 'The most famous, most fearsome MONSTER of all!'?

BUT THEN BLIND RAGE SWELLED UP IN ME, AND IN THAT INSTANT I SPRANG FROM MY HIDING PLACE...

GROWRRR!

OH NO! DEAR LORD-- NOOOOOO!!!

HER SCREAMS FOR PITY AND SALVATION WENT UNHEARD AS I HURTLED THROUGH THE WINDOW AND THREW MYSELF UPON HER! THOUGHT HAD NO PLACE IN ME NOW... AND IN PLACE OF THE WOMAN I SAW ONLY THE SOURCE OF ALL THINGS VILE AND LOATHSOME IN THE HUMAN RACE

The panel on the left shows the moment when the creature kills Dr Frankenstein's fiancée.

3 What is the effect of allowing the monster to tell his own story?

4 How does this monster differ from the monster of the films?

5 How similar does he seem to the creature of Mary Shelley's novel?

6 Do you know of any other green-skinned comic book monsters that are ugly on the outside but are really quite sensitive?

7 If the monster is at the centre of the story, what role is Dr Frankenstein likely to play?

E SPEAKING AND LISTENING   READING   WRITING

More recent incarnations of the monster have included a comic version in *Young Frankenstein* (he learns to tap-dance and sing), a friendly version in *The Munsters* and an authentic version in *Mary Shelley's Frankenstein*, a film version made in 1994. Creatures that return to attack their creators occur in many other films and stories, most notably in Ridley Scott's *Blade Runner*.

With a partner, discuss what you think is the appeal of this type of story.

● What does it say about human nature?
● What does it say about the role of the scientist?
● Why do audiences keep returning to these themes?

Review

As a class, discuss the following.

● How much should any film that calls itself *Frankenstein* reflect the contents of Mary Shelley's novel?
● How little needs to be included for the film to qualify as an adaptation of the book?
● Do you think the changing interpretations of the scientists and creatures in the adaptations you have discussed reflect changes in attitudes to exclusion and the power of scientists?

Points of view

Aims

- To look at how an author's standpoint can affect meaning.

Starter session

With a partner, work out how many ways you can say the following sentences to give them slightly different meanings.

- Nice dress. - I'm sorry. - If you don't mind. - Do you think so? - Great!

Introduction

In speech, we can often change the meaning of what we say by changing our tone of voice. In writing, it is much more difficult to establish **tone** (but not, of course, impossible).

Discuss with a partner how you would describe the tone of the following statements.

No one could accuse the Beckhams of being publicity shy.

If you want to advertise your Britishness, there is nothing better than wearing a pair of sandals and knee-length socks.

The house was absolutely fabulous, full of the most gorgeous furniture and an astonishing collection of paintings.

I suppose I might be able to drag myself out at the weekend.

KEY WORD

The **tone** of speech or writing describes its overall quality. For instance, a song might have a mournful tone or a political speech might have an optimistic tone.

Development

In the following article Miranda Sawyer is discussing 'reality TV' programmes, but in the course of it she also attacks middle-class attitudes. Read the article carefully and then answer the questions that follow.

Keeping it real

The only problem the middle classes have with reality TV is that it's far too … real.

Miranda Sawyer

Reality TV gets a rotten press, but before so-called ordinary people were allowed to be themselves in front of a camera, telly was as dull as Noel Edmonds's ditchwater. Week after week, it presented us with drama that was less dramatic than our own lives, with comedy that wasn't as funny, with presenters who made the dumbest of our mates look like a walking, talking Stephen Hawking. Television fitted neatly into its place, the corner of the cosy lounge, by offering us consistent comfort viewing. We watched it for its soothing nature, its reassuring, sausage-and-mash attitudes. Don't worry about this changing world, cooed Big Mother in the corner, for in telly time, everything is always the same: tall men in specs are funny; large-chested women won't come to any good; posh people are cruel and/or sexually frustrated; the working classes like a sing-song when drunk.

You could tell it was dull because whenever telly showed honest emotion, it exploded right through the small screen, as if it had jumped out of the set to land splat!, all over the rug. What a mess. And it was almost always by mistake: George Best drunk and indiscreet on Wogan […]. Even now, we remember the Stone Roses calling The Old Grey Whistle Test 'amateurs', Oliver Reed trying to snog a feminist on After Dark, Tracey Emin waving her broken finger at the Turner Prize, Keith Allen losing his rag and walking off-set mid-interview. Why? Because such events were shocking, memorable. Proper tears, genuine anger and sloppy drunkenness are mesmerising when they're on the small screen, because real lives and real emotion are far too messy, far too big for the controlled, small environment of the livest of live TV.

Which is why, when Jerry Springer came along, the middle classes – the self-appointed policemen of our nation's moral standards – decided it was A Terrible Thing. It's all very well for celebrities to make fools of themselves, but all these awful, common people, with their awful, common lives, shouting and hitting and getting at and getting off with each other! Who let them into our quiet little party? Shouldn't they be on a council estate, or in therapy, or jail, or somewhere – anywhere – away from our front room? The same people got upset with docusoaps. Hardly Reithian* values, they sniffed, unaware that maybe they could learn from these splashy, bright, entertaining personalities. If they're not being lectured at by someone with a degree, or a regular slot on a Radio Four panel show, the middle classes really are unteachable.

So when 'reality TV' smeared itself all over our screens, it was all their worst fears realised. Hours and hours of these dreadful people, in all their mixed-up glory. Why would you want to watch that? Don't you get enough of it at home? But, of course, reality TV isn't real life. It's real people but in fantasy situations, whether uncomfortable (*Big Brother*), unusual (*The 1940s House*) or full of opportunity (*Popstars*). How great is that?

Only morons would want to appear on a reality show, sniff the bourgeoisie, who would rather die than wash their dirty knickers in public, let alone be shown crying over a verruca. But, in a country where opportunities are still so skewed that we boast Europe's highest property prices at the same time as one of its highest child-poverty levels, it doesn't

strike me as moronic. How else are you going to get to taste the wonder of money, the excitement of having your picture in the paper, the challenge of living on a tropical island? And who else but Ground Force or Trinny and Tranny are going to do up your house or wardrobe for free?

There has, rightly, been a furore over a TV company's decision to pay for Ryan Williams, a problem teenager from Wandsworth, to attend a private boarding school. Of course, Ryan should have been catered for within our public-education system. But he wasn't. No wonder he grabbed his opportunity.

No one else, apart from telly, would have helped him. There will be even more outrage when, during the next US presidential election, a Big Brother-style interactive elimination show chooses a candidate. But why is that so much worse than having multinational corporations choosing one? At least regular voters will be involved in the political process. And how else would an ordinary person ever get anywhere near national politics? If our systems offered a mere fraction of the opportunities of reality TV, we'd all be better off.

* Reithian – typical of Lord Reith, the first director general (1927–38) of the BBC. He believed that television should have a moral and educational role.

The tone of an article can often be affected by word choice.

1 What message about her own sympathies does Miranda Sawyer give by using the words 'rotten', 'telly', 'dull as … ditchwater', 'our mates', 'sausage-and-mash attitudes', 'specs', 'posh' and 'sing-song' in the first paragraph?

2 What other examples of colloquial language can you find in the article?

3 What attitude towards television companies is shown by her use of the words 'cosy', 'comfort viewing', 'cooed' and 'Big Mother' in the first paragraph?

4 What image of middle-class life and values do the words in Question 3 conjure up?

On a number of occasions Miranda Sawyer imagines what middle-class people might say.

5 She uses the words 'sniff' and 'sniffed' to describe middle-class speech. How does this make middle-class people appear?

6 She also makes them describe the working classes as 'awful' and 'common' people who should be 'on a council estate, or in therapy, or jail.' What is her overall attitude to the middle classes?

7 Does Miranda Sawyer provide any evidence that middle-class people actually expressed the views she ascribes to them?

8 How would you describe her writing about the middle classes?

When she is writing about reality TV, Miranda Sawyer shows a very different attitude.

9 Pick out the negative words in the fourth paragraph. Now pick out the positive words. Whose view is represented by the negative words? What is Miranda Sawyer's own view?

The last three paragraphs have a more serious tone.

10 Read the sentence that begins on line 7 of the fifth paragraph. How would you describe the author's use of the word 'boast' here?

11 What real benefits for ordinary people does Miranda Sawyer describe in the fifth and sixth paragraphs?

12 Is Miranda Sawyer being serious when she says that reality TV will help democracy in America?

B **SPEAKING AND LISTENING** READING WRITING

With a partner, discuss the way in which this article develops. It was published in *The Observer*, which is a newspaper mostly read by middle-class people. How do you think *Observer* readers would have reacted to the first part of the article? Do you think they would agree with the last three paragraphs?

Review

As a class, discuss Miranda Sawyer's use of tone and underlying attitudes in this article. Do you think it is successful in making its point about the failings of British society and middle-class snobbery? The tone is quite light-hearted and a little cynical. Would a serious essay about the positive benefits of reality TV programmes have been just as good?

Homework

Either: Write a brief account of how Miranda Sawyer gives the impression that she is writing from a working-class point of view but also signals that she is really middle-class. Use evidence from the article.

or: Write your own article defending something unpopular using some of the techniques demonstrated by Miranda Sawyer.

Aristotle and advertising

Aims

- To analyse and discuss how advertisements make use of **rhetorical devices**.

Starter session

KEY WORDS

One of the most well-known **rhetorical devices** is the **rhetorical question**. A rhetorical question is asked for a purpose other than to obtain the information being requested (e.g. Shall we begin? Do you really want to do that? That's not very clever, is it?).

Rhetorical questions can:

- help to persuade
- express emotions
- make an audience feel well-disposed towards the speaker.

1 Copy out the table below. Fill in the purpose of each question: is it designed to persuade, express emotion, or make you feel well-disposed towards the speaker?

Question	Purpose
How would you like to have your house bombed?	
Why are you so clever?	
Why me, Lord?	
Is that the time?	
Isn't it about time you got rid of that old sofa?	
Shall I pour?	

2 Write a further six **rhetorical questions** of your own and ask a partner to decide on the purpose of each one.

Introduction

According to the philosopher Aristotle (384–322 BC), who wrote one of the earliest and most influential books on the subject, the art of rhetoric is the art of persuasion. He said that there are three main elements to persuading people. These are:

- **Logos** (words). This refers to the intellectual or informative parts of an argument. Aristotle says that this ought to be the most convincing aspect, but because of human nature, frequently it isn't.
- **Ethos** (people). This refers to the perceived qualities of the person doing the persuasion. Is he or she trustworthy/well-informed/well-intentioned?
- **Pathos** (emotion). According to Aristotle, arousing people's feelings is often the most powerful persuasive technique.

Development

 SPEAKING AND LISTENING   **READING**   WRITING

Logos

Facts and figures can be persuasive, but they are not very exciting in an advertisement. Look at these two advertisements for a car and a computer. With a partner, discuss the following.

1 Why have the car manufactures concentrated on pathos, as expressed in the picture, as opposed to logos, as expressed in the information at the bottom of the page?

2 Why have the advertisers of the computer concentrated on logos?

3 What do these two advertisements tell you about how people decide to buy cars or computers?

Pathos

The Benetton clothing company is famous for using pathos in its advertisements. On the right is an example from their poster campaigns.

1 With your partner, discuss the emotions that the picture is meant to arouse.

2 How do you think that people are meant to respond to such images being used to advertise clothing?

3 What do you think about Benetton as a result of seeing this picture?

The Benetton company is unusual in using such shocking images. Often, advertisers use emotions such as greed, envy or sexual desire as a way to sell their products.

4 Identify the emotion being used in each of the ads shown here. Write a brief account of how the emotion is communicated through words and pictures.

5 In groups, discuss which part of an advertisement communicates emotion most effectively – the words or the pictures.

Ethos

Ethos is probably one of the most complex parts of persuasion in advertising and involves such things as:

- using pictures of famous people in ads
- employing well-known people for voice-overs
- using people who look like experts to present a product
- sponsoring well-known sportsmen and women or performers
- employing people with particular accents to talk about a product.

1 Employing famous people is very expensive for advertisers. Why do you think they are prepared to pay so much money for a famous person to advertise their product?

2 Why do you think there are so many telephone call centres in Scotland?

3 Why do advertisers put actors in white coats to talk about products such as toothpaste on television?

4 What problems might occur if a company pays a great deal of money to sponsor an artist? How might this have an impact on the artist's work?

5 Do you think the fact that someone famous uses a product actually tells you anything about the product?

Now Made with Pure Sunflower Oil for 33% Less Fat but 100% Taste

Review

In this unit we have looked at rhetorical techniques used by advertisers that date back over 2,000 years. These techniques – logos, pathos and ethos – relate to our intellect, our emotions and how we feel about other people, and are therefore very powerful. As a class, brainstorm as many current ads as you can and identify which of the three techniques each of them uses.

Homework

Either: Demonstrate your understanding of logos, pathos and ethos by designing an advertisement that uses all three. Write a brief description explaining how you have employed the three rhetorical techniques.

or: Find an example of an advertisement and identify its main persuasive technique as either logos, ethos or pathos. Write a brief account of how the technique is used. Take your work into school and make a wall display in which advertisements are placed under the three main categories. Which persuasive technique is the most popular?

Year 9 SATs

I Join the Regiment

Lugging a suitcase tied with traditional knotted string, I made my way to Headquarters 56th Heavy Regiment Royal Artillery. Using sign language they re-directed me to D Battery. They were stationed in a building called 'Worthingholm', an evacuated girls' school in Hastings Road. As I entered the drive, a thing of singular military ugliness took my eye. It was Battery Sergeant-Major 'Jumbo' Day. His hair was so shorn his neck seemed to go straight up the back of his hat, and his face was suffused red by years of drinking his way to promotion.

'Oi! Where yew goin'? It ain't a girls' school no more.'

'Isn't it? Never mind I'll join the Regiment instead,' I said.

He screwed up his eyes. 'You're not Milligan, are yew?'

'Actually I am.'

A beam of sadistic pleasure spread over his face.

'We've been waiting for yew!' he said, pushing me ahead of him with his stick. He drove me into what was D Battery Office. The walls once white were now thrice grey. From a peeling ceiling hung a forty watt bulb that when lit made the room darker. A Janker Wallah was giving the bare floor a stew-coloured hue by slopping a mop around, re-arranging the dirt. Fronting the fireplace was a trestle table covered with a merry grey blanket. A pile of O.H.M.S. letters, all addressed to me, were tucked in the corner of the blotter. In the lid of a cardboard shoe-box was a collection of rubber bands, paper-clips, sealing-wax, string and a lead weight. My pulses raced! Here was the heart of a great fighting machine. Seated behind this mighty war organ was a middle-aged, pink, puffy-faced man in his early fifties wearing a uniform in its late seventies. Parts that had frayed had been trimmed with leather; these included cuffs, elbows, pockets, gaiters and all trailing edges; for this reason he was known as 'Leather Suitcase'. His maiden name was Major Startling-Grope. 'This is Gunner Milligan sir,' said the B.S.M. When they'd both finished laughing, the Major spoke.

'Whair hev yew been, and whai are yew wearing civilian clothes?'

'They wouldn't let me on the train naked sir.'

'I mean, whai aren't you in uniform?'

'I'm not at war with anybody sir.'

'Silence when you speak to an officer,' said B.S.M.

The Major, who was fiddling with a rubber band, slid it over his finger.

'Does this mean we're engaged sir?'

'Silence!' said B.S.M.

'I suppose,' said Suitcase, 'you know you are three months late arriving?'

'I'll make up for it sir, I'll fight nights as well!' All these attempts at friendly humour fell on stony ground. I was marched to a bare room by a Bombardier. He pointed to a floor board.

'You're trying to tell me something,' I said.

'Your bed, right?'

'Right.'

'Right Bombardier!'

'I'm a Bombardier already?'

'Oh, cheeky bastard, eh? Got the very job for yew.'

He gave me a scrubbing-brush with two bristles, showed me a three acre cook-house floor and pointed down; he was still trying to tell me something. Leering over all this was the dwarf-like Battery Cook, Bombardier Nash, who looked like Quasimodo with the hump reversed. He was doing things to sausages. Three hours' scrubbing, and the knees in my trousers went through. To make matters worse there were no uniforms in the 'Q' stores. I cut a racy figure on guard, dark blue trousers gone at the knee, powder blue double-breasted chalk-stripe jacket, lemon shirt and white tie, all set off with steel helmet, boots and gaiters. It wasn't easy.

From Adolf Hitler, My Part in his downfall

Spike Milligan

Pages 27–29

Michael Joseph 1971

Penguin Books 1972

© Spike Milligan Productions 1971

Dambusters, 21st March 1943

617 Squadron was formed by Wing Commander Guy Gibson on 21 March 1943 from selected crews in 5 Group and the squadron trained for 6 weeks for this special operation. 19 Lancasters were dispatched in 3 waves, each aircraft armed with the special bouncing bomb developed by Barnes Wallis for attacking German dams. The entire operation was to be carried out at low level to escape attack from German night fighters and to release the bombs just above the water in the dams.

One aircraft had to return early after it struck the sea a glancing blow, which tore off its bomb. 5 further aircraft were shot down or crashed before reaching their targets and 1 was so badly damaged by Flak that it had to turn back. This left 12 Lancasters available to bomb the dams. Wing Commander Gibson's aircraft and 4 other crews bombed the Mohne Dam and breached it despite intense fire from light Flak defending the dam. 3 aircraft went on to bomb the Eder Dam, which was also breached. 2 aircraft bombed the Sorpe Dam and 1 the Schwelme Dam but without causing breaches in their walls. The twelfth surviving aircraft could not find its target in misty conditions and returned to England without dropping its bomb. 3 further Lancasters were shot down after they had bombed.

Total casualties were 8 aircraft out of the 19 dispatched. It is estimated that 4 were shot down by light Flak, 1 crashed after being damaged by the explosion of its own bomb, 2 crashed after hitting electricity cables and 1 after striking a tree when its pilot was dazzled by a searchlight. Of the 56 crew members in these planes, 53 were killed and only 3 became prisoners of war, 2 of them being badly injured. For his leadership of this amazing operation and for his courage in attacking Flak positions at the Mohne Dam after having carried out his own bombing run, Wing Commander Gibson was awarded the Victoria Cross. 34 other men received decorations.

The breaching of the Mohne and Eder Dams were major achievements. The Mohne reservoir contained nearly 140 million tons of water and was the major source of supply for the industrial Ruhr 20 miles away. The water released caused widespread flooding and disruption of rail, road and canal communications and of the supply of electricity and water. The water-supply network was particularly affected by the silting up of pumping stations by the flood water. It is not possible to state the effect of all this upon industrial production in precise terms but there was certainly some disruption and water rationing was in force until the winter rains came and filled the reservoirs again.

The Eder was even larger than the Mohne, containing 210 million tons of water, but it was 60 miles from the Ruhr. The city of Kassel, 25 miles away, and the inland waterway system in the Kassel area, were more affected by the attack on the Eder than was the Ruhr area. The German view is that, if the aircraft, which were allocated to the Eder had been switched to the Sorpe Dam, the effect upon the Ruhr's industrial production would have been extremely serious, but the Sorpe's construction was of a nature which made it a difficult target for the Wallis bomb, hence its low priority in the raid. The Sorpe reservoir just managed to keep the Ruhr supplied with water until the Mohne Dam was repaired.

The number of people drowned has been calculated at 1,294 most of them near the Mohne Dam. The town of Neheim-Husten, which was situated 5 miles downstream of the Mohne Dam, took the full impact of the flood and at least 859 people died there. It is believed that 58 or more of the dead were around the Eder Dam. The total number of dead as quoted at 1,294.

Year 9 Test Questions

Answer the following questions in your books.

Questions 1–4 are about *I join the regiment*.

1 Why is Milligan in trouble with the sergeant major and his commanding officer? *(1 mark)*

2 What two reasons does Milligan give for not being in uniform? *(1 mark)*

3 How does the writer show the difference between himself and the officers in the dialogue?

  a Pick out two examples which show how the officers speak. *(1 mark)*

  b How is Milligan's speech different from the officers'? *(1 mark)* c How do these differences affect the reader's response to Milligan and the officers? *(1 mark)*

4 In the whole text, how does the writer give a sense of the pettiness and silliness of war?
You should comment on how the writer:
- uses conversation
- uses illogical and surreal images
- contrasts what is happening with the wider issue of a serious war. *(5 marks)*

Questions 5–8 are about *Dambusters*.

5 From paragraph 2, give two reasons why some of the bombers failed to reach their target. *(2 marks)*

6 From paragraph 4, sum up the effects of the bombing of the Mohne dam. *(2 marks)*

7 In the whole text show how the writer tries to present the bravery of the men who went on the mission while being honest about its effects. *(5 marks)*

8 Wing Commander Guy Gibson is mentioned three times in the text. Give two reasons why you think he has been picked out for special mention. *(2 marks)*

Question 9 is about *I Join the Regiment* and *Dambusters*.

9 I Join the Regiment and Dambusters are very different texts.
Copy out and complete the table below, suggesting:
- one purpose of each text
- one word or phrase to describe the language used in each text.

	I join the Regiment	*Dambusters*
Purpose of text		
Language used in the text		

(2 marks)